IC OCEAN

EUROPE
pages 32 – 37

ASIA
pages 44 – 49

AFRICA
pages 38 – 43

PACIFIC

OCEAN

EQUATOR

INDIAN

OCEAN

AUSTRALIA
pages 50 – 55

ANTARCTICA
pages 56 – 59

NATIONAL GEOGRAPHIC

BEGINNER'S World Atlas

NATIONAL GEOGRAPHIC
WASHINGTON, D.C.

Photographs from Getty Images

NATIONAL GEOGRAPHIC

BEGINNER'S World Atlas

Table of Contents

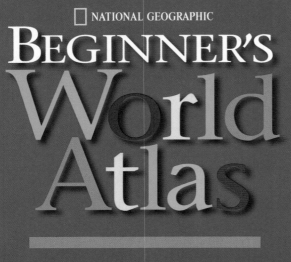

What Is a Map?

A map is a drawing of a place as it looks from above. It is flat, and it is smaller than the place it shows. A map can help you find where you are and where you want to go.

Mapping Your Backyard...

...from the ground

From your backyard you see everything in front of you straight on. You have to look up to see your roof and the tops of trees. You can't see what's in front of your house.

...from higher up

From higher up you look down on things. You can see the tops of trees and things in your yard and in the yards of other houses in your neighborhood.

Finding places on the map

A **map** can help you get where you want to go. A map tells you how to read it by showing you a compass, a key, and a scale.

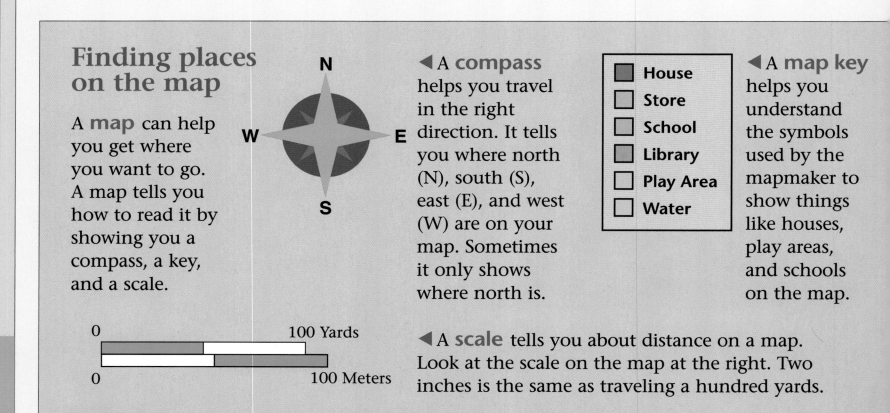

◄A **compass** helps you travel in the right direction. It tells you where north (N), south (S), east (E), and west (W) are on your map. Sometimes it only shows where north is.

■	House
□	Store
□	School
■	Library
□	Play Area
□	Water

◄A **map key** helps you understand the symbols used by the mapmaker to show things like houses, play areas, and schools on the map.

◄A **scale** tells you about distance on a map. Look at the scale on the map at the right. Two inches is the same as traveling a hundred yards.

0   100 Yards

0   100 Meters

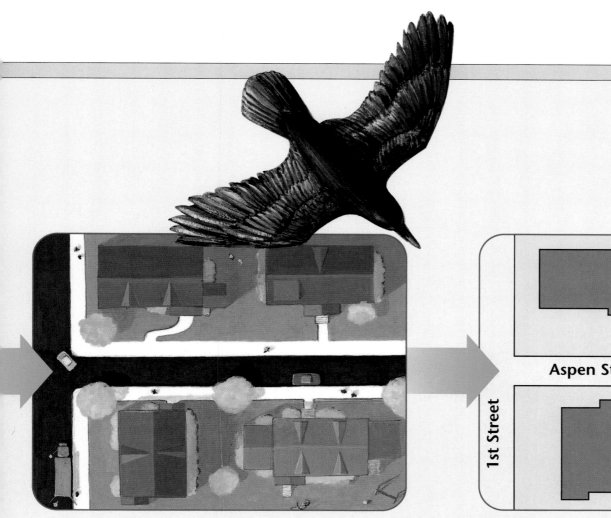

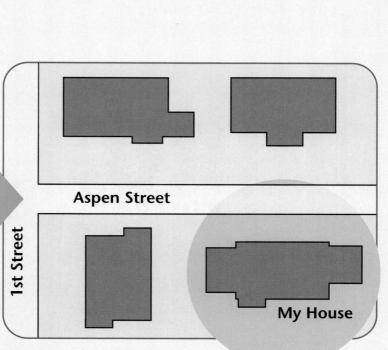

...from a bird's-eye view

If you were a bird flying directly overhead, you would see only the tops of things. You wouldn't see walls, tree trunks, tires, or feet.

...on a map

A map looks at places from a bird's-eye view. But it uses drawings called symbols to show things that don't move, such as houses.

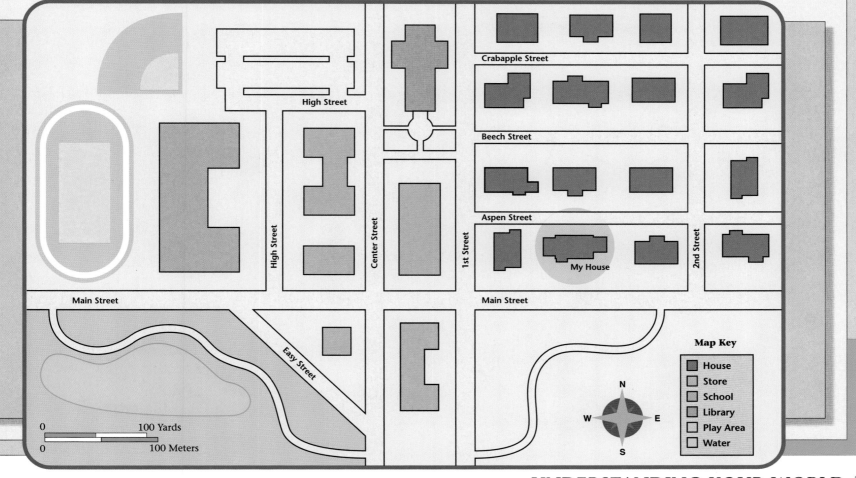

Making the Round Earth Flat

From your backyard Earth probably looks flat. If you could
travel into space like an astronaut, you would see that Earth
is a giant ball with blue oceans, greenish-brown land, and white
clouds. Even in space you can only see the part of Earth facing
you. To see the whole Earth at one time you need a map.
Maps take the round Earth and make it flat so you can
see all of it at one time.

▼ Earth in Space

From space you can see that Earth is
round with oceans, land, and clouds.
But you can see only half of
Earth at one time.

**NORTH
AMERICA**

EQUATOR

▼ Earth on Paper

If you could peel a globe like an orange, you could make Earth flat, but there would be spaces between the pieces. Mapmakers stretch the land and the water at the top and bottom to fill in the spaces. This is how a **map** lets you see the whole world all at once.

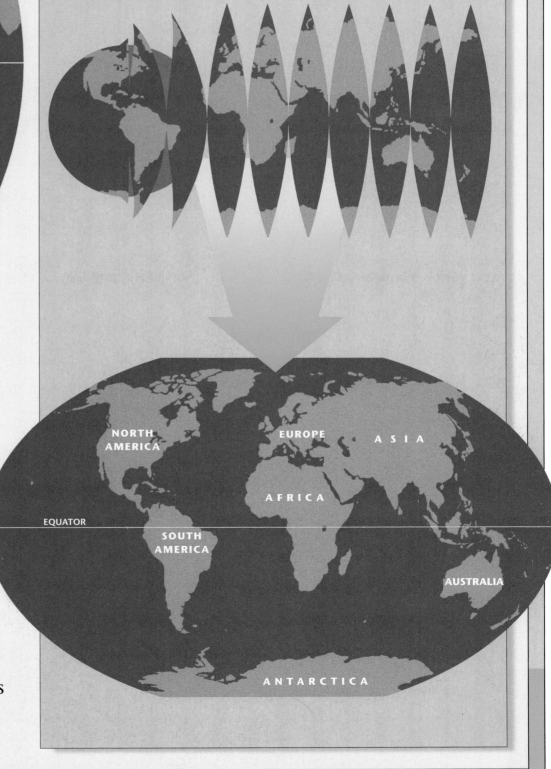

SOUTH AMERICA

NORTH AMERICA

EUROPE

ASIA

AFRICA

EQUATOR

SOUTH AMERICA

AUSTRALIA

ANTARCTICA

▲ Earth as a Globe

A **globe** is a tiny model of Earth that you can put on a stand or hold in your hand. You have to turn it to see the other side. You still can't see the whole Earth at one time.

The **Equator** is an imaginary line around Earth's middle. Mapmakers show it as a solid or a dashed line on globes and maps.

The Physical World

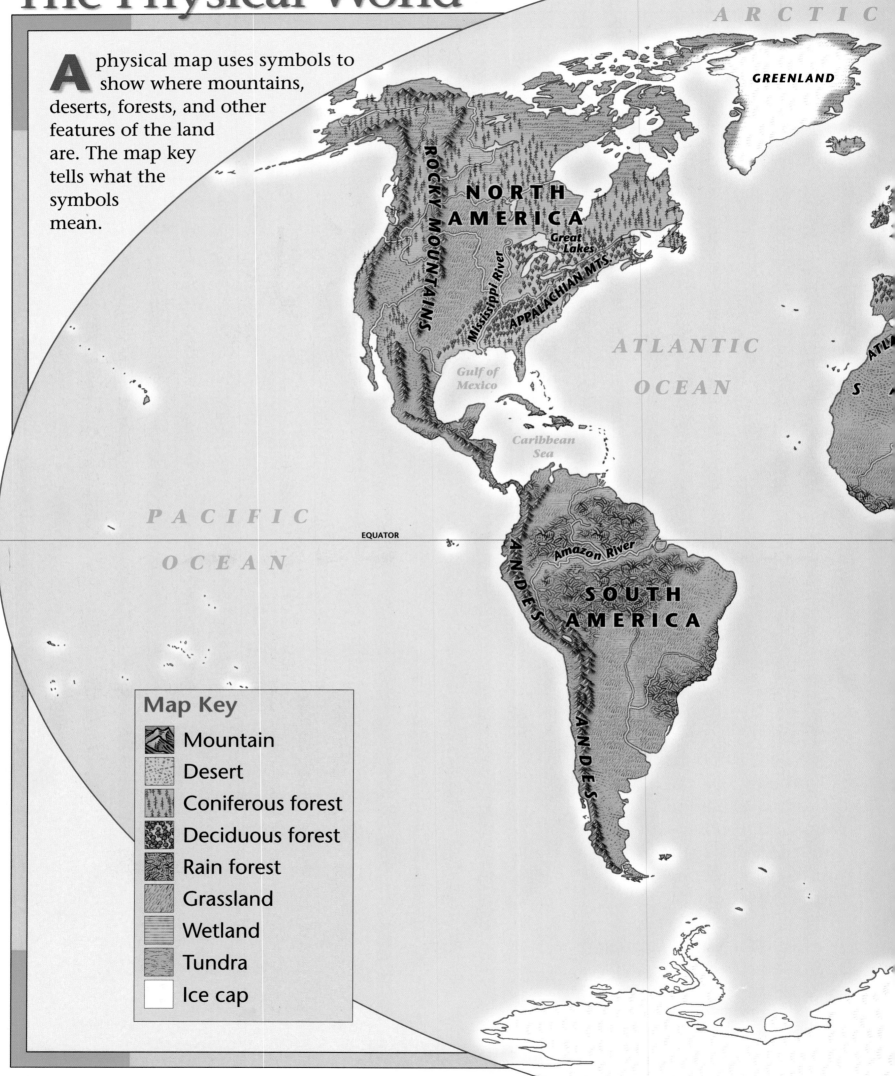

A physical map uses symbols to show where mountains, deserts, forests, and other features of the land are. The map key tells what the symbols mean.

ARCTIC

GREENLAND

NORTH AMERICA

ROCKY MOUNTAINS

Great Lakes

Mississippi River

APPALACHIAN MTS.

Gulf of Mexico

Caribbean Sea

ATLANTIC OCEAN

ATLANTIC

S

PACIFIC OCEAN

EQUATOR

Amazon River

ANDES

SOUTH AMERICA

ANDES

Map Key

- Mountain
- Desert
- Coniferous forest
- Deciduous forest
- Rain forest
- Grassland
- Wetland
- Tundra
- Ice cap

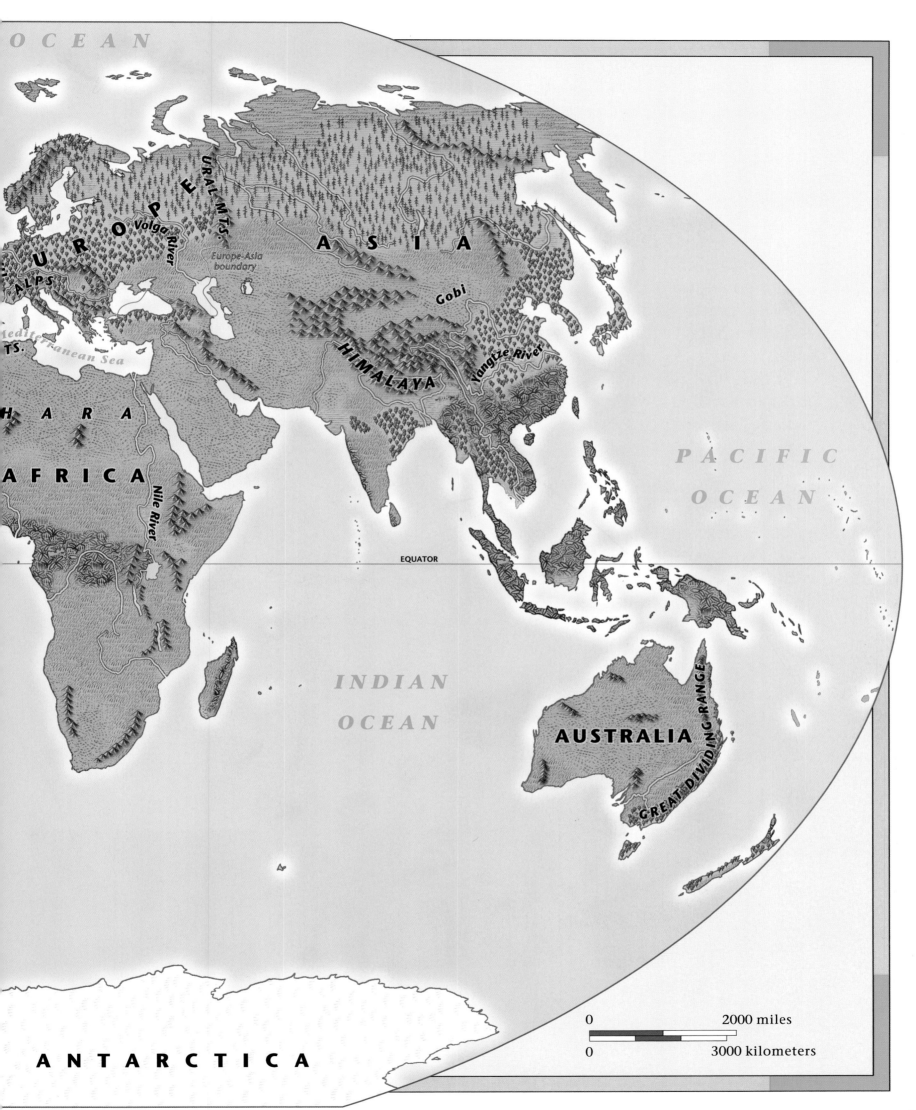

O C E A N

EUROPE

URAL Mts.

Volga River

Europe-Asia boundary

ALPS

Mediterranean Sea

TS.

HARA

AFRICA

Nile River

ASIA

Gobi

HIMALAYA

Yangtze River

PACIFIC OCEAN

EQUATOR

INDIAN OCEAN

AUSTRALIA

GREAT DIVIDING RANGE

A N T A R C T I C A

0   2000 miles

0   3000 kilometers

The Physical World Close Up

The Earth's surface is made up of land and water. The biggest landmasses are called **continents**. All seven of them are named on this map. **Islands** are smaller pieces of land that are surrounded by water. Greenland is the largest island. Land that is almost entirely surrounded by water is called a **peninsula**. Europe has lots of them.

Oceans are the largest bodies of water. Can you find all four oceans? **Lakes** are bodies of water surrounded by land—like the Great Lakes, in North America. A large stream of water that flows into a lake or an ocean is called a **river**. The Nile is Earth's longest river.

These are Earth's main physical features. But continents also have mountains, deserts, forests, and many other kinds of physical features. The **map symbols** below show the features that will appear on the physical maps in this atlas. Each symbol is followed by a brief description that explains its meaning. There is also a photograph so you can see what each feature looks like in the real world.

Each continent has different kinds of features, so each physical map will have its own map key.

Mountain
Land that rises at least 1,000 feet above the surrounding land

Desert
Very dry land that can be hot or cold and sandy or rocky

Coniferous forest
Forest with trees that have seed cones and often needlelike leaves

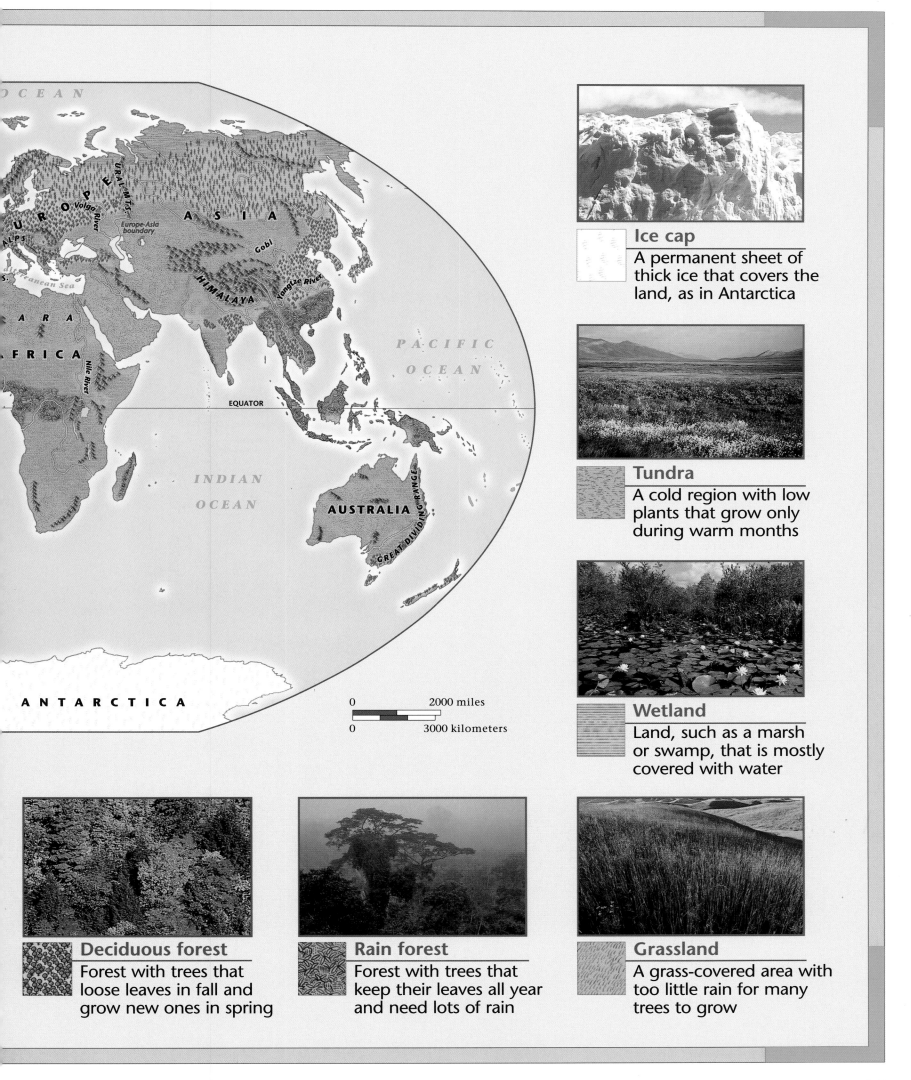

Ice cap

A permanent sheet of thick ice that covers the land, as in Antarctica

Tundra

A cold region with low plants that grow only during warm months

Wetland

Land, such as a marsh or swamp, that is mostly covered with water

Deciduous forest

Forest with trees that loose leaves in fall and grow new ones in spring

Rain forest

Forest with trees that keep their leaves all year and need lots of rain

Grassland

A grass-covered area with too little rain for many trees to grow

The Political World

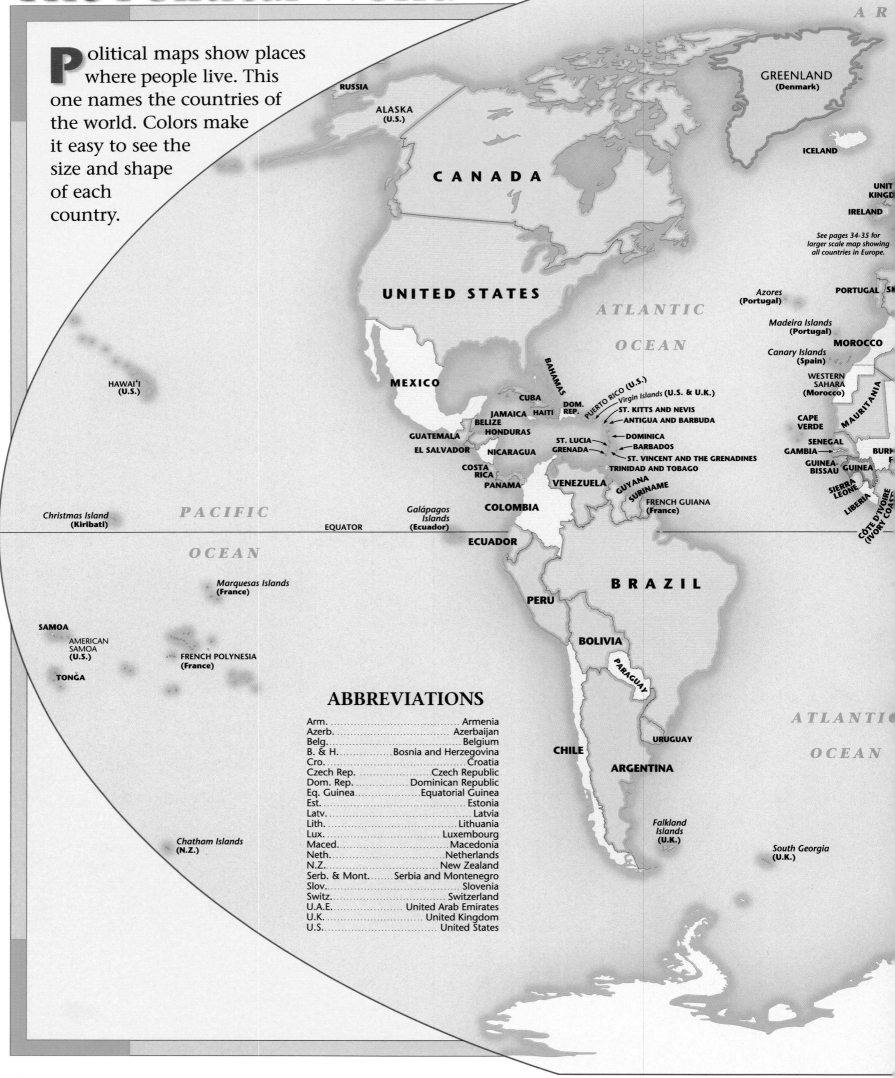

Political maps show places where people live. This one names the countries of the world. Colors make it easy to see the size and shape of each country.

RUSSIA

GREENLAND
(Denmark)

ALASKA
(U.S.)

ICELAND

C A N A D A

UNIT
KINGD

IRELAND

See pages 34-35 for larger scale map showing all countries in Europe.

UNITED STATES

ATLANTIC

OCEAN

*Azores
(Portugal)*

PORTUGAL SI

*Madeira Islands
(Portugal)*

MOROCCO

HAWAI'I
(U.S.)

MEXICO

BAHAMAS

CUBA

DOM.
REP.

PUERTO RICO (U.S.)

Virgin Islands (U.S. & U.K.)

ST. KITTS AND NEVIS

ANTIGUA AND BARBUDA

*Canary Islands
(Spain)*

WESTERN
SAHARA
(Morocco)

CAPE
VERDE

MAURITANIA

JAMAICA HAITI

BELIZE

GUATEMALA

HONDURAS

DOMINICA

BARBADOS

SENEGAL

S',

EL SALVADOR

ST. LUCIA

GRENADA

NICARAGUA

ST. VINCENT AND THE GRENADINES

TRINIDAD AND TOBAGO

GAMBIA

GUINEA-
BISSAU

GUINEA

BURK
F

COSTA
RICA

PANAMA

VENEZUELA

GUYANA

SURINAME

SIERRA
LEONE

LIBERIA

*Christmas Island
(Kiribati)*

PACIFIC

EQUATOR

*Galápagos
Islands
(Ecuador)*

COLOMBIA

FRENCH GUIANA
(France)

CÔTE D'IVOIRE
(IVORY COAST)

OCEAN

ECUADOR

*Marquesas Islands
(France)*

B R A Z I L

PERU

SAMOA

AMERICAN
SAMOA
(U.S.)

FRENCH POLYNESIA
(France)

BOLIVIA

PARAGUAY

TONGA

ATLANTI

OCEAN

URUGUAY

CHILE

ARGENTINA

*Chatham Islands
(N.Z.)*

*Falkland
Islands
(U.K.)*

*South Georgia
(U.K.)*

ABBREVIATIONS

Arm.	Armenia
Azerb.	Azerbaijan
Belg.	Belgium
B. & H.	Bosnia and Herzegovina
Cro.	Croatia
Czech Rep.	Czech Republic
Dom. Rep.	Dominican Republic
Eq. Guinea	Equatorial Guinea
Est.	Estonia
Latv.	Latvia
Lith.	Lithuania
Lux.	Luxembourg
Maced.	Macedonia
Neth.	Netherlands
N.Z.	New Zealand
Serb. & Mont.	Serbia and Montenegro
Slov.	Slovenia
Switz.	Switzerland
U.A.E.	United Arab Emirates
U.K.	United Kingdom
U.S.	United States

A R

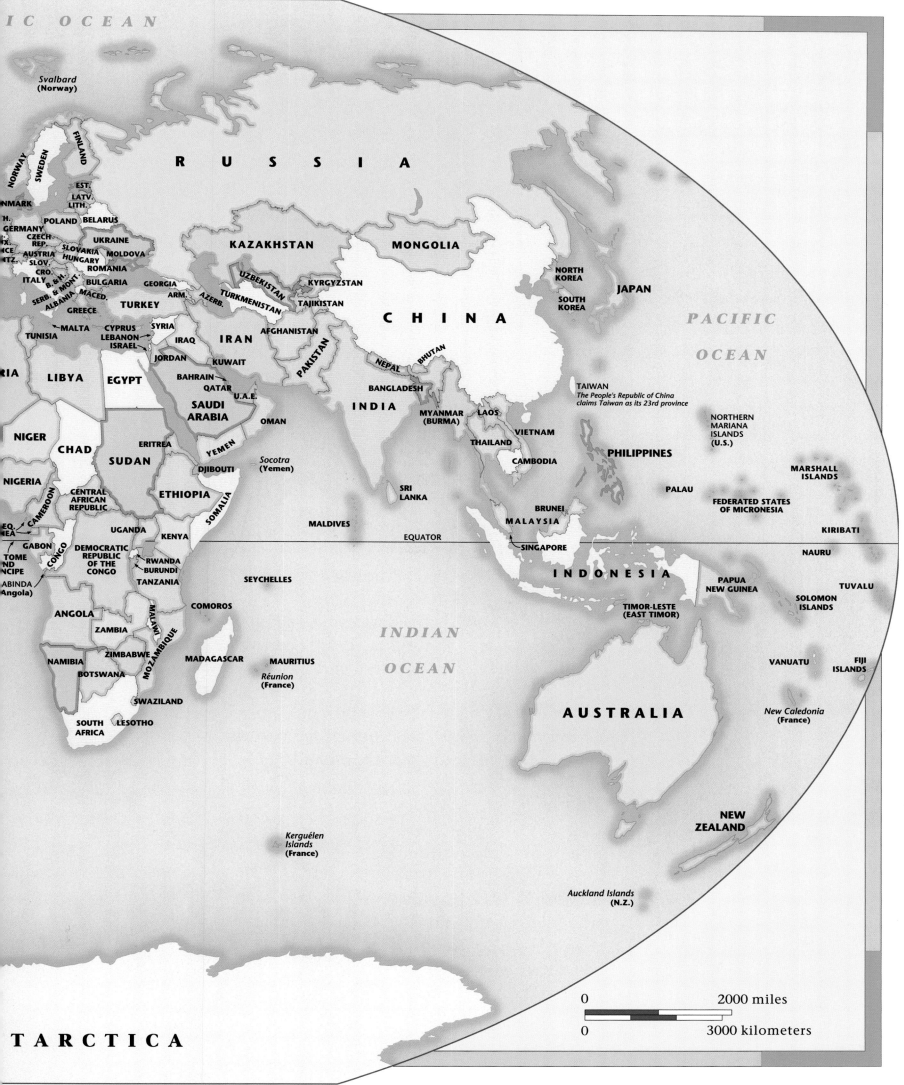

IC *OCEAN*

Svalbard
(Norway)

NORWAY
SWEDEN
FINLAND

R U S S I A

EST.
LATV.
LITH.

NMARK

POLAND BELARUS

H.
GERMANY
CZECH
REP. UKRAINE
AUSTRIA SLOVAKIA MOLDOVA
NCE SLOV. HUNGARY
TZ. CRO. ROMANIA
ITALY B.&H.
SERB. & MONT. BULGARIA
ALBANIA MACED.
GREECE **TURKEY**

KAZAKHSTAN

MONGOLIA

NORTH
KOREA

JAPAN

SOUTH
KOREA

GEORGIA
ARM.
AZERB. UZBEKISTAN KYRGYZSTAN
TURKMENISTAN TAJIKISTAN

TUNISIA MALTA CYPRUS
LEBANON SYRIA
ISRAEL

C H I N A

PACIFIC

OCEAN

RIA **LIBYA** **EGYPT** IRAQ **IRAN**
JORDAN KUWAIT
BAHRAIN AFGHANISTAN
QATAR
U.A.E.

PAKISTAN

NEPAL BHUTAN

TAIWAN
*The People's Republic of China
claims Taiwan as its 23rd province*

NIGER

CHAD

**SAUDI
ARABIA**

OMAN

BANGLADESH

I N D I A

MYANMAR
(BURMA) LAOS

NORTHERN
MARIANA
ISLANDS
(U.S.)

ERITREA

YEMEN

THAILAND

VIETNAM

PHILIPPINES

NIGERIA

SUDAN

DJIBOUTI

*Socotra
(Yemen)*

CAMBODIA

MARSHALL
ISLANDS

CENTRAL
AFRICAN
REPUBLIC

ETHIOPIA

SOMALIA

SRI
LANKA

PALAU

FEDERATED STATES
OF MICRONESIA

EQ.
NEA CAMEROON

UGANDA

KENYA

MALDIVES

BRUNEI

MALAYSIA

KIRIBATI

GABON
TOME
ND
NCIPE

DEMOCRATIC
REPUBLIC
OF THE
CONGO

RWANDA
BURUNDI

CONGO

TANZANIA

EQUATOR

SINGAPORE

NAURU

ABINDA
Angola)

SEYCHELLES

I N D O N E S I A

PAPUA
NEW GUINEA

TUVALU

ANGOLA

ZAMBIA

COMOROS

TIMOR-LESTE
(EAST TIMOR)

SOLOMON
ISLANDS

NAMIBIA

ZIMBABWE

MALAWI

MADAGASCAR

MAURITIUS

INDIAN

MOZAMBIQUE

BOTSWANA

*Réunion
(France)*

OCEAN

VANUATU

FIJI
ISLANDS

SWAZILAND

SOUTH
AFRICA LESOTHO

AUSTRALIA

*New Caledonia
(France)*

*Kerguélen
Islands
(France)*

**NEW
ZEALAND**

*Auckland Islands
(N.Z.)*

TARCTICA

0   2000 miles

0   3000 kilometers

What This Atlas Will Teach You

Y ou hold the world in your hands as you look through the pages of this atlas. You will find a physical and a political map of each continent. Here is what you will learn about each one.

Mountains, Asia

THE PHYSICAL WORLD

 Land regions You will find out what kinds of land cover a continent. Does it have mountains and deserts? If so, where are they?

 Water You will learn about a continent's chief lakes, rivers, and waterfalls. You'll see that some continents have more water than others.

 Climate Climate is the weather of a place over many years. Some continents are colder and wetter or hotter and drier than others.

 Plants You'll discover what kinds of plants grow on a particular continent.

Animals Continents each have certain kinds of animals. Did you know that tigers live in the wild only in Asia?

Coral reef, Pacific Ocean

Desert, North America

Camels, India

Vancouver, Canada

Grapes, Mediterranean region

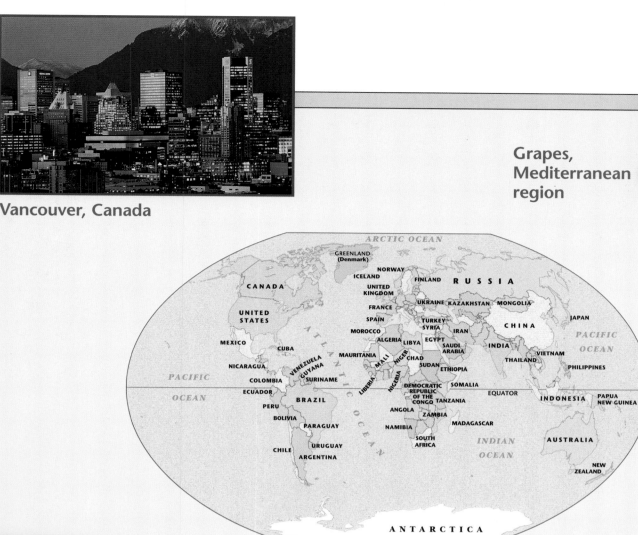

THE POLITICAL WORLD

Eurostar train, Europe

Countries You will learn about the countries that make up a continent. Maps show country names in type like this: **UNITED STATES**

Cities You will find out which are the most important cities on a continent. The map key will tell you which cities are country capitals.

People You will learn where groups of people on a continent come from, where they live, what they do, how they have fun, and more.

Eiffel Tower, France

Languages Many languages are spoken on most continents. Here you will find out which languages most people speak.

Schoolgirls, Vietnam

Products This section will tell you which goods produced on a continent are most important to the people living there.

North America

N orth America is shaped like a triangle ▼. It is wide in the north. In the south it becomes a strip of land so narrow that a Marathon runner could cross it in two hours. Ships make the trip on the Panama Canal. The warm islands in the Caribbean Sea are part of North America. So is icy Greenland in the far north. The seven countries between Mexico and South America make up a region commonly called Central America. It connects the rest of North America and South America.

Kha-hay! I'm from the Crow tribe in Montana. This beautiful valley is in Yosemite National Park, in California. It's in the Sierra Nevada mountains. Look for it on the map when you turn the page.

North America

The Land

Mt. McKinley (Denali)
Highest elevation in North America

Land regions The Rocky Mountains run along the west side of North America through Mexico. There, the mountains are called the Sierra Madre Oriental. Lower mountains called the Appalachians are in the east. Grassy plains lie between the two mountain chains.

▲ North America is famous for its **deciduous forests**. Leaves turn fiery colors each fall!

Water Together the Mississippi and the Missouri make up the longest river. The Great Lakes are the world's largest group of freshwater lakes.

▲ A white-tailed deer nuzzles her babies in a meadow near the **Great Lakes.** Deer live in almost every country on the continent.

Climate The far north is icy cold. Temperatures get warmer as you move south. Much of Central America is hot and wet.

◄ Palm trees grow along sandy beaches on islands in the **Caribbean Sea.** In this part of North America the weather is warm year-round.

Plants North America has large forests where there is plenty of rain. Grasslands cover drier areas.

Animals There is a big variety of animals—everything from bears, moose, and wolves to monkeys and colorful parrots.

▼ **Deserts** are found in the southwestern part of North America. The large rock formation on the right is called The Mitten. Can you guess why?

◄ Dragonlike iguanas live in the **rain forests** of Mexico and Central America. This harmless lizard can grow as long as a man's leg.

ASIA

ARCTIC OCEAN

GREENLAND

Brooks Range

kon River

Mackenzie River

Great Bear Lake

Great Slave Lake

Hudson Bay

R O C K Y

Columbia River

G R E A T   M O U N T A I N S

Lake Winnipeg

Great Lakes

Missouri River

Sierra Nevada

Colorado River

G R E A T   P L A I N S

Mississippi River

Ohio River

Appalachian Mountains

Death Valley owest elevation in North America

SIERRA MADRE OCCIDENTAL

Rio Grande

SIERRA MADRE ORIENTAL

PACIFIC OCEAN

Gulf of Mexico

ATLANTIC OCEAN

W E S T

I N D I E S

Caribbean Sea

CENTRAL AMERICA

SOUTH AMERICA

▲ This view from a plane shows that **Greenland** has high mountains and lots of snow and ice.

Map Key

- Mountain
- Desert
- Coniferous forest
- Deciduous forest
- Rain forest
- Grassland
- Wetland
- Tundra
- Ice cap

0   600 miles

0   900 kilometers

North America

The People

 Countries Canada, the United States, Mexico, and the countries of Central America and the West Indies make up North America.

Cities Mexico City is the biggest city in North America. Next in size are New York City and Los Angeles. Havana, in Cuba, is the largest city in the West Indies.

People Ancestors of most people in North America came from Europe. Many other people trace their roots to Africa and Asia. Native Americans live throughout the continent.

Languages English and Spanish are the main languages. large number of people in Canada and Haiti speak French. There are also many Native American languages.

Products North America's chief products include cars, machinery, petroleum, natural gas, silver, wheat, corn, beef, and forest products.

▲ Skiing and ski jumping are popular sports in the **Rocky Mountains.**

▲ This farmer is harvesting wheat on a big farm in **Canada.** Canada and the United States grow much of the world's wheat.

▲ This is **Mexico City.** More people live here than in any other city in North America.

▲ This pyramid at **Chichén Itzá** was built long ago by the Maya people.

◄ These red berries hold coffee beans. Many farmers in **Guatemala** make a living growing coffee.

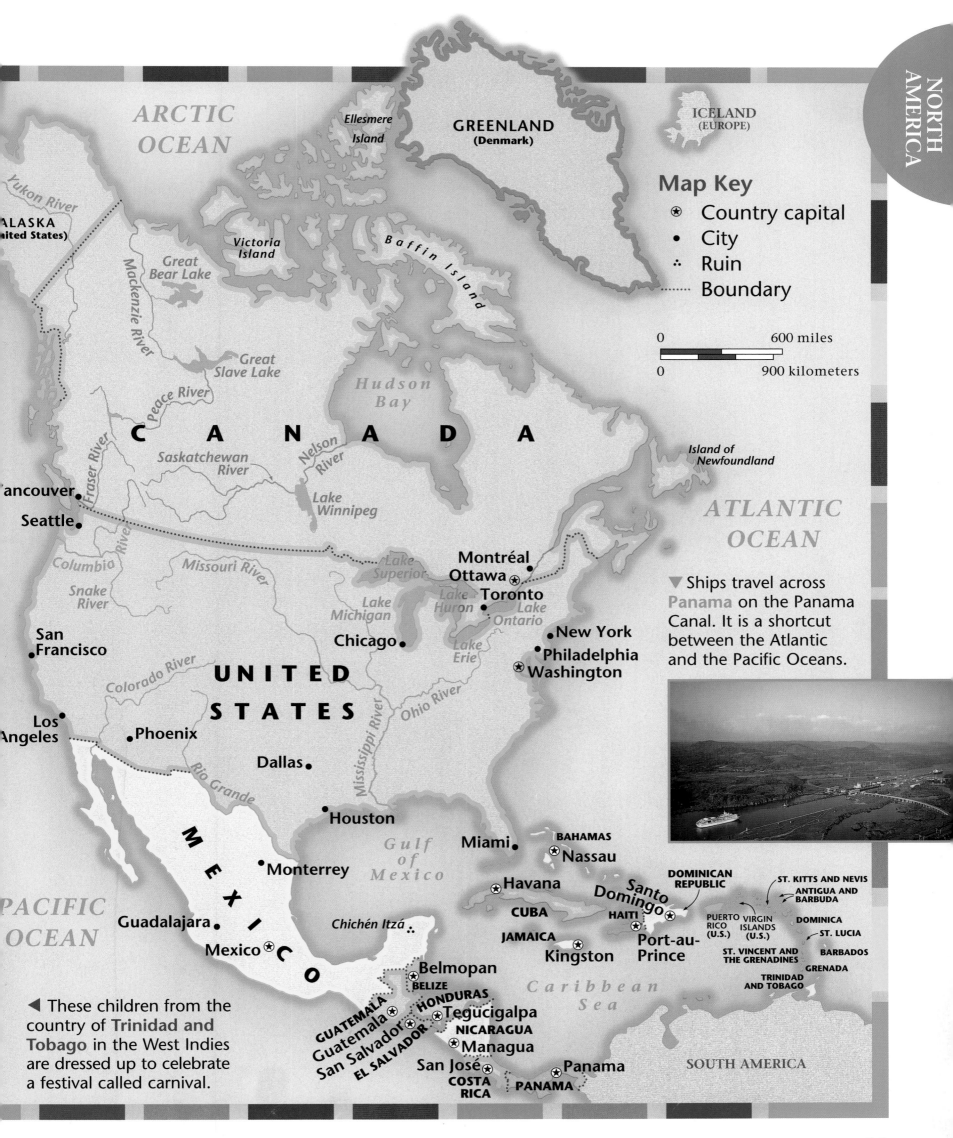

ARCTIC OCEAN

Yukon River

ALASKA (United States)

GREENLAND (Denmark)

Ellesmere Island

ICELAND (EUROPE)

Map Key
- ⊛ Country capital
- • City
- ∴ Ruin
- ..... Boundary

0   600 miles

0   900 kilometers

Victoria Island

Great Bear Lake

Baffin Island

Mackenzie River

Great Slave Lake

Peace River

Hudson Bay

C A N A D A

Fraser River

Saskatchewan River

Nelson River

Island of Newfoundland

Vancouver

Seattle

Lake Winnipeg

ATLANTIC OCEAN

Columbia River

Missouri River

Lake Superior

Montréal

Ottawa ⊛

Toronto

Lake Huron

Lake Ontario

▼ Ships travel across **Panama** on the Panama Canal. It is a shortcut between the Atlantic and the Pacific Oceans.

Snake River

Lake Michigan

Chicago

Lake Erie

New York

Philadelphia

⊛ Washington

San Francisco

U N I T E D

S T A T E S

Colorado River

Los Angeles

Phoenix

Mississippi River

Ohio River

Dallas

M E X I C O

Houston

Miami

BAHAMAS

⊛ Nassau

Gulf of Mexico

Monterrey

⊛ Havana

Santo Domingo

DOMINICAN REPUBLIC

ST. KITTS AND NEVIS

ANTIGUA AND BARBUDA

PACIFIC OCEAN

Guadalajara

Chichén Itzá

CUBA

HAITI

PUERTO RICO (U.S.)

VIRGIN ISLANDS (U.S.)

DOMINICA

ST. LUCIA

Mexico ⊛

JAMAICA

Kingston ⊛

Port-au-Prince

ST. VINCENT AND THE GRENADINES

BARBADOS

GRENADA

Belmopan

BELIZE

Caribbean Sea

TRINIDAD AND TOBAGO

◄ These children from the country of **Trinidad and Tobago** in the West Indies are dressed up to celebrate a festival called carnival.

GUATEMALA

Guatemala

San Salvador

EL SALVADOR

HONDURAS

⊛ Tegucigalpa

NICARAGUA

⊛ Managua

San José ⊛

COSTA RICA

⊛ Panama

PANAMA

SOUTH AMERICA

United States

The People

▲ Chinese New Year is a big celebration in **San Francisco**. Lots of Chinese live there.

States The United States is made up of 50 states. Alaska and Hawai'i are separated from the rest of the country. So you can see them close up, they are shown near the bottom of the map. Use the small globe to see their real locations.

Cities Washington, D.C., is the national capital. Each state also has a capital city. New York City has the most people.

People People from almost every country in the world live in the United States. Most live and work in and around cities.

▲ Sandy beaches, like this one in **Delaware**, are popular places to visit in the summer.

Languages English is the chief language, followed by Spanish.

Products The chief products include cars, machinery, petroleum, natural gas, coal, beef, wheat, and forest products.

▶ Baseball is a popular sport in the United States along with soccer, basketball, and football. This girl lives in **California**.

Seattle
Olympia
WASHINGTON
Portland
Salem
OREGON
Boise
IDAHO
C A L I F O R N I A
Sacramento
Carson City
NEVADA
Salt La
C
San Francisco
San Jose
Las Vegas
Los Angeles
ARI
Phoen
San Diego
Tucson

PACIFIC OCEAN

ALASKA

Juneau

0   400 miles
0   600 kilometers

Honolulu

HAWAI'I

0   150 miles
0   200 kilometers

CANADA

Missouri River

MONTANA
Helena

NORTH DAKOTA
⊙ Bismarck

MINNESOTA

MICHIGAN

Lake Superior

Lake Ontario

MAINE
⊙ Augusta

Montpelier ⊙
VT. N.H.
⊙ Concord

NEW YORK
Albany ⊙

⊙ Boston
MASS.
⊙ Providence
CONN. RHODE ISLAND

SOUTH DAKOTA
⊙ Pierre

WISCONSIN
Minneapolis ● St. Paul ⊙
Milwaukee ●
Madison ⊙

Rochester ●
Buffalo ●

Hartford ⊙

WYOMING

Lansing ⊙
Detroit ●
Cleveland ●
Pittsburgh ●

PENNSYLVANIA
Harrisburg ⊙

New York ●
Trenton ⊙
NEW JERSEY
Philadelphia ●

NEBRASKA
Omaha ●
Lincoln ⊙

IOWA
⊙ Des Moines

Chicago ●

ILLINOIS
INDIANA
Indianapolis ⊙

OHIO
Columbus ⊙

Baltimore ●
MARYLAND
DELAWARE
Dover ⊙

Cheyenne ⊙

Colorado River

Denver ⊙
COLORADO

Springfield ⊙

Cincinnati ●

⊙ Annapolis
★ Washington, D.C.

WEST VIRGINIA
⊙ Charleston

Richmond ⊙

Santa Fe ⊙

Topeka ⊙
Kansas City ●
Jefferson City ⊙
St. Louis ●

Frankfort ⊙

VIRGINIA

KANSAS
Wichita ●

MISSOURI

KENTUCKY

Raleigh ⊙

Nashville ⊙
NORTH CAROLINA
Charlotte ●

Albuquerque ●
NEW MEXICO

Tulsa ●
OKLAHOMA
Oklahoma City ⊙

ARKANSAS
Little Rock ⊙

TENNESSEE
Memphis ●

SOUTH CAROLINA
⊙ Columbia

El Paso ●

Forth Worth ● ● Dallas

Jackson ⊙
MISSISSIPPI

Atlanta ⊙
● Birmingham
ALABAMA
⊙ Montgomery

GEORGIA
● Savannah

TEXAS
Austin ⊙
Houston ●
● San Antonio

LOUISIANA
Baton Rouge ⊙ ● New Orleans

Tallahassee ⊙
FLORIDA

Jacksonville ●

Orlando ●

Rio Grande

Tampa ●

Miami ●

Gulf of Mexico

MEXICO

ATLANTIC OCEAN

This bridge is in **New York City**. The Empire State Building stands tall against the sky.

Map Key

⊛ Country capital
⊙ State capital
● City
⋯⋯ Boundary

0 ——— 400 miles

0 ——— 600 kilometers

◀ A scarecrow stands guard over a field of sunflowers in **Kansas**.

▶ Spicy boiled crawfish are a favorite dish in **Mississippi** and other states that border the Gulf of Mexico.

Canada

The People

Provinces Canada is divided into ten provinces and three territories. Nunavut is a brand-new homeland for Eskimos. The largest number of people live in Ontario and Quebec.

Cities Ottawa is Canada's capital. Toronto, Montreal, and Vancouver are among its largest cities and ports.

People Canada has fewer people than the state of California. Most Canadians live within a hundred miles of the country's southern border. The territories have a lot of land but very few people.

Languages Canada's street signs are often in two languages. That's because English and French are the chief languages. Most French-speaking Canadians live in Quebec.

Products Canada's chief products include cars, forest products, petroleum, natural gas, aluminum, nickel, iron ore, beef, and wheat.

▲ Royal Canadian Mounted Police often perform their famous Musical Ride in Ottawa.

▲ Banff, in Alberta, is one of several national parks in the Rocky Mountains of western Canada.

ARCTIC O

Beaufort Sea

ALASKA (U.S.)

YUKON TERRITORY

Mackenzie River

Great Bear Lake

Yukon River

⊙ Whitehorse

NORTHW TERRITOR

Yellowknif

C

BRITISH COLUMBIA

Peace River

Fraser River

ALBERT

Edmonton ⊙

Vancouver Island

• Vancouver

Calga

Victoria ⊙

PACIFIC OCEAN

▼ During Canada's long, cold winters, ice hockey is a popular sport. The Hockey Hall of Fame is in Toronto, Ontario.

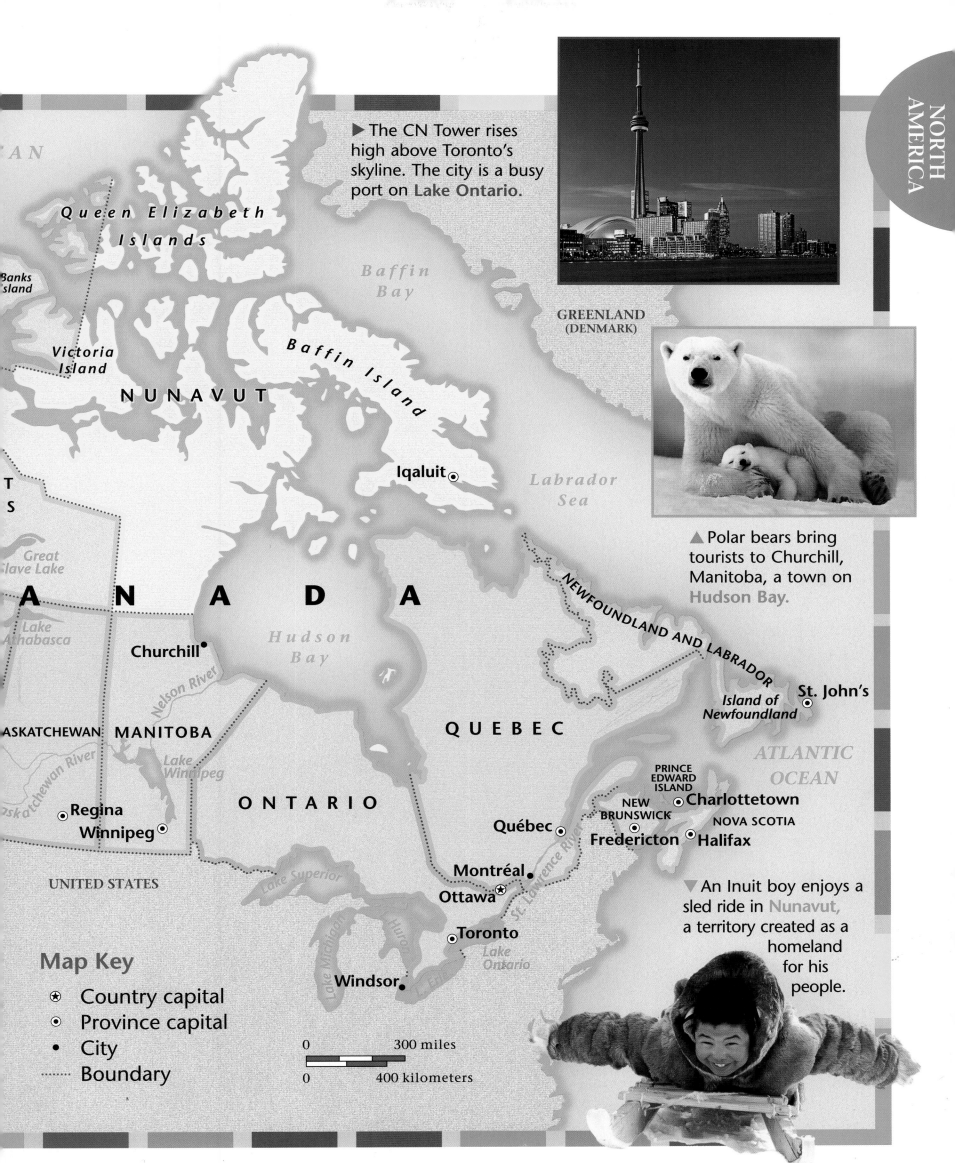

Queen Elizabeth
Islands

Banks
Island

Baffin
Bay

► The CN Tower rises
high above Toronto's
skyline. The city is a busy
port on Lake Ontario.

GREENLAND
(DENMARK)

Victoria
Island

NUNAVUT

Baffin Island

Great
Slave Lake

Iqaluit ⊙

Labrador
Sea

▲ Polar bears bring
tourists to Churchill,
Manitoba, a town on
Hudson Bay.

CANADA

Hudson
Bay

NEWFOUNDLAND AND LABRADOR

St. John's

Lake
Athabasca

Churchill •

Nelson River

Island of
Newfoundland

ASKATCHEWAN MANITOBA

QUEBEC

ATLANTIC
OCEAN

askatchewan River

Lake
Winnipeg

PRINCE
EDWARD
ISLAND

Charlottetown ⊙

Regina ⊙
Winnipeg ⊙

ONTARIO

NEW
BRUNSWICK

NOVA SCOTIA

Québec ⊙

Fredericton ⊙ Halifax ⊙

UNITED STATES

Lake Superior

St. Lawrence River

Montréal •

▼ An Inuit boy enjoys a
sled ride in Nunavut,
a territory created as a
homeland
for his
people.

Ottawa ⊛

Lake Michigan

Lake Huron

Toronto ⊙
Lake
Ontario

Map Key

⊛ Country capital

⊙ Province capital

• City

······ Boundary

Windsor •

Lake Erie

| 0 | 300 miles |
| 0 | 400 kilometers |

South America

Visit South America, and you will see many wonderful things. It has the world's biggest rain forest and one of the driest deserts. It has emerald mines, mysterious ruins, and crowded modern cities with glass-and-steel skyscrapers. In the mountains, camel-like animals called llamas are trained to carry goods. On the grasslands, cowboys called gauchos round up cattle. You might be surprised to learn that some familiar foods, such as potatoes and tomatoes, are native to South America.

Imaynalla! Greetings in Quechua, my native language. I live in the mountains of Peru. Do you like my market-day outfit? Behind me is Iguazú Falls, one of the world's largest waterfalls. It's on the border between Argentina and Brazil.

South America

The Land

![mountain icon] **Land regions** Snowcapped mountains called the Andes run along the whole west coast. Rain forests and grasslands cover much of the rest of the continent. The continent's driest desert lies between the Andes and the Pacific Ocean.

![water icon] **Water** The Amazon River carries more water than any other river in the world. More than 1,000 streams and rivers flow into it. Lake Titicaca, in the Andes, is the continent's largest lake.

![sun icon] **Climate** Much of South America is warm all year. The coldest places are in the Andes and at the continent's southern tip. Each year about 80 inches of rain falls in the rain forests.

![leaf icon] **Plants** The Amazon rain forest has more kinds of plants than any other place in the world. Grasslands feed large herds of cattle and sheep.

![turtle icon] **Animals** Colorful macaws, noisy howler monkeys, and giant snakes live in the rain forest. Sure-footed llamas, huge birds called condors, and guinea pigs live in the Andes. The flightless rhea, which looks like an ostrich, roams the wide southern grasslands.

▲ Cold outside and hot inside, snow-covered **volcanoes** are scattered throughout the Andes.

► The world's largest water lilies grow in the **Amazon River.** They are big enough to hold a child.

▲ The **Atacama**, in northern Chile, is one of the world's driest deserts.

▼ Imagine living in a place where birds are as big and as colorful as these macaws. They live in the **rain forest.**

Lake
Maracaibo

Orinoco
River

A M A Z O N

Negro River

Amazon River

Amazon River

EQUATOR

A N D E S

B A S I N

Lake Titicaca

Atacama Desert

Paraguay River

Paraná River

Iguazú
Falls

Paraná River

Mt. Aconcagua
*Highest elevation in
South America*

A N D E S

Río de la Plata

PACIFIC

OCEAN

Valdés Peninsula
*Lowest elevation in
South America*

ATLANTIC

OCEAN

▲ Llamas are camel-like animals
that live in the **Andes.**

Map Key

Mountain

Desert

Rain forest

Grassland

Wetland

| 0 | | 600 miles |
| 0 | | 900 kilometers |

Falkland
Islands

Strait of Magellan

South America

The People

◄ Many bananas sold in the United States and other countries come from **Ecuador**. Check the label the next time you go to the store!

Countries South America has just 12 countries—French Guiana is not really a country because it belongs to France. All but two of these countries border an ocean. Can you find these two countries on the map?

Cities Most of the largest cities are near the oceans. São Paulo, in Brazil, is South America's biggest city. Bolivia has two capital cities: La Paz and Sucre.

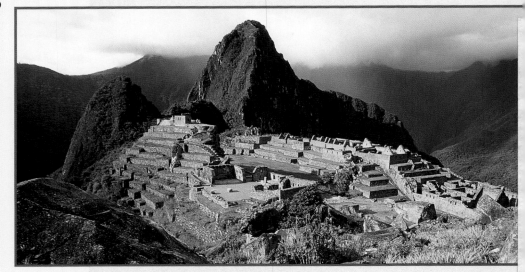

▲ Long ago, the Inca people built the city of **Machu Picchu** high in the Andes of Peru.

People The native people came from the north long ago. Colonists came from Europe, especially from Spain and Portugal. They brought African slaves to work in the fields. Most people in South America are descendants of these three groups.

► Soccer is the most popular sport in South America. This famous player, known as Pelé, is from **Brazil**.

Languages Spanish and Portuguese are the continent's chief languages. Indians speak Quechua and other native languages.

Products South America's chief products include bananas, cattle, coffee, copper, emeralds, oranges, and sugar.

◄ This man plays his guitar to entertain people on the streets of **Buenos Aires**, in Argentina. Guitar music is popular in South America.

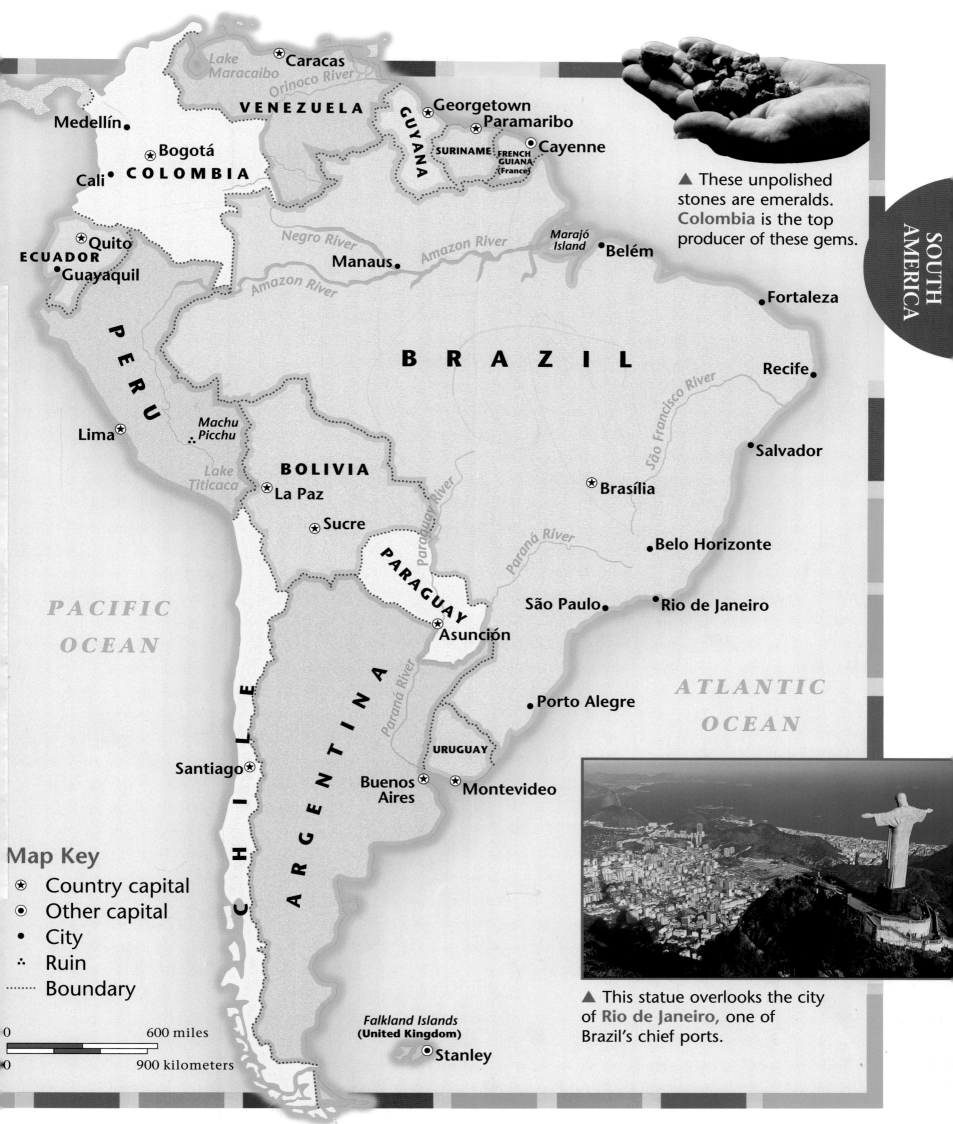

Caracas

Lake Maracaibo

Orinoco River

VENEZUELA

Medellín

Bogotá

Cali

COLOMBIA

ECUADOR

Quito

Guayaquil

GUYANA

Georgetown

Paramaribo

SURINAME

Cayenne

FRENCH GUIANA (France)

▲ These unpolished stones are emeralds. **Colombia** is the top producer of these gems.

SOUTH AMERICA

Negro River

Amazon River

Manaus

Marajó Island

Belém

Fortaleza

Amazon River

P E R U

Machu Picchu

Lima

Lake Titicaca

BOLIVIA

La Paz

Sucre

B R A Z I L

São Francisco River

Recife

Salvador

Brasília

Belo Horizonte

Paraguay River

PARAGUAY

Asunción

Paraná River

São Paulo

Rio de Janeiro

PACIFIC OCEAN

ATLANTIC OCEAN

Paraná River

Porto Alegre

URUGUAY

Santiago

Buenos Aires

Montevideo

C H I L E

A R G E N T I N A

Map Key

⊛ Country capital

⊙ Other capital

• City

∴ Ruin

...... Boundary

0   600 miles

0   900 kilometers

Falkland Islands (United Kingdom)

Stanley

▲ This statue overlooks the city of **Rio de Janeiro,** one of Brazil's chief ports.

Europe

Travel through the countryside in Europe and you might think you have wandered into the pages of a storybook. You'll see castles, cuckoo clocks, and cobblestone streets. But Europe is also one of the most modern continents. You can ride one of the world's fastest trains through a tunnel beneath the English Channel, watch sports cars being made in Italy, and visit famous museums in Paris. On a map Europe may look like it is part of Asia, but it is considered to be a separate continent.

Sveiks! I'm from Latvia, a country on the Baltic Sea. I am wearing a costume for a dance. Wouldn't you like to visit this town in Austria? It's on a lake high in the Alps, Europe's highest mountains.

Iceland

Europe

▲ People often try to climb the **Matterhorn**. It is one of the highest peaks in the Alps.

Land regions Europe's most obvious feature is its coastline, cut with bays and peninsulas of every size. The Alps are high mountains that form a chain across much of southern Europe.

Water Several large rivers flow across Europe. Some of the most important include the Danube, Rhine, Volga, and Rhône.

Climate Warm winds from the Atlantic Ocean help give most of Europe a mild climate. This climate plus plenty of rain makes much of Europe good for farming.

▲ Much of Europe is farmland. Fields of lavender grow in the mild climate east of the **Rhône**. Perfume is made from these flowers.

Plants Europe's largest forests are in the north. Cork and olive trees grow along the Mediterranean Sea.

Animals Reindeer are common in the far north. Many kinds of goatlike animals live in the Alps. Robins, nightingales, and sparrows are among Europe's native birds.

► This is a kind of wild goat called an ibex. It is one of many kinds of hooved animals that live in the **Alps** and other mountainous parts of the continent.

ATLANTIC OCEAN

Ireland

Great Britain

PYRENEES

IBERIAN PENINSULA

M

```
0                    600 miles
|___|___|___|___|___|___|
0                    900 kilometers
```

AFRICA

► Europe has many sandy beaches on the **Mediterranean Sea**. The most famous are along the coast, in Italy and France.

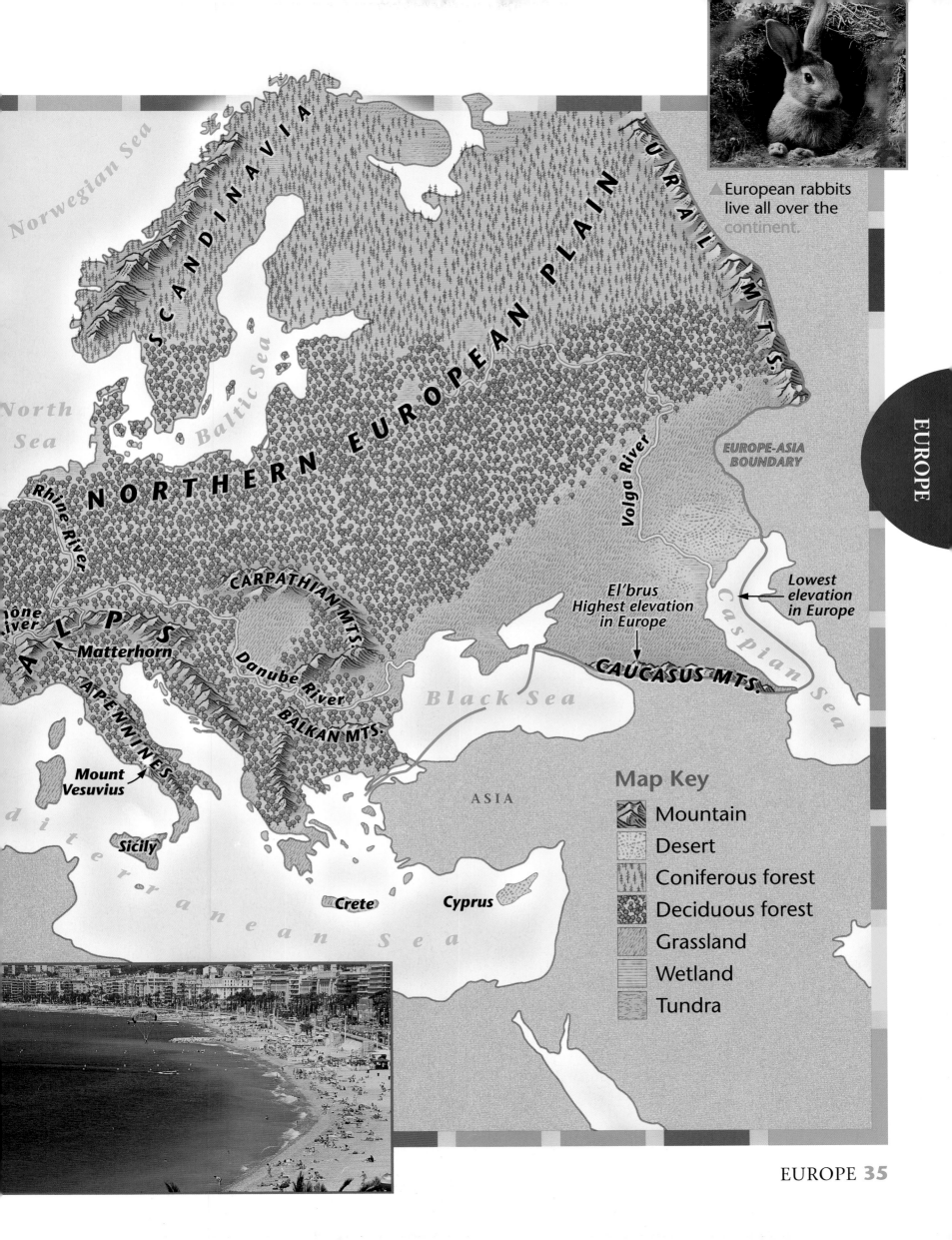

Norwegian Sea

North Sea

Baltic Sea

SCANDINAVIA

NORTHERN EUROPEAN PLAIN

URAL MTS.

▲ European rabbits live all over the continent.

EUROPE

EUROPE-ASIA BOUNDARY

Volga River

Rhine River

ALPS

Rhône River

Matterhorn

CARPATHIAN MTS.

Danube River

BALKAN MTS.

APENNINES

Mount Vesuvius

Sicily

Black Sea

El'brus
Highest elevation in Europe

CAUCASUS MTS.

Caspian Sea

Lowest elevation in Europe

ASIA

Crete

Cyprus

Mediterranean Sea

Map Key

🗻	Mountain
	Desert
	Coniferous forest
	Deciduous forest
	Grassland
	Wetland
	Tundra

Europe

The People

(see pages 48–49)

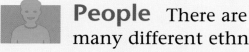
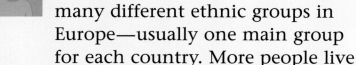

Countries There are 44 countries in Europe. Even though most of Russia is in Asia *(see pages 48–49)*, the country is usually counted as being part of Europe. There are five island countries: Iceland, United Kingdom, Ireland, Malta, and Cyprus.

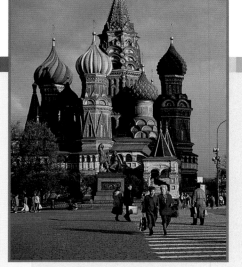

▲ St. Basil's is a famous Russian orthodox church. It is in **Moscow**, Russia's capital city.

Cities Most cities in Europe are within a few hundred miles of the sea. London, in the United Kingdom, is Europe's largest city.

People There are many different ethnic groups in Europe—usually one main group for each country. More people live in cities than on farms.

▲ Bagpipe music is popular in Scotland, which was once an independent country. Today, Scotland is part of the **United Kingdom.**

Languages About 50 languages are spoken in Europe, including English, French, German, and Russian. Many Europeans speak more than one language.

Products Europe's chief products include iron, coal, petroleum, cars, machinery, wheat, fruit, and olives.

▼ People gather to hear the pope speak in **Vatican City,** the world's smallest country. It is surrounded by the city of Rome.

◄ The euro is currently the official money in **Italy** and 11 other members of the European Union *(see page 61).*

ATLANTIC OCEAN

Reykjavík ✳ **ICELAND**

Faroe Islands (Denmark)

Orkney Islands

Edinburgh

IRELAND
Dublin ✳

UNITED KINGDOM

London ✳

English Channel

FRANCE

Bordeaux

PORTUGAL

Lisbon ✳

ANDORRA

✳ Madrid

SPAIN

Seville

Balearic Islands (Spain)

GIBRALTAR (U.K)

Paris

AFRICA

Map Key

- ⊛ Country capital
- • City
- ⋯⋯ Boundary

EUROPE-ASIA BOUNDARY

| 0 | 600 miles |
| 0 | 900 kilometers |

Norwegian Sea

Shetland Islands

Oslo ⊛

Stockholm ⊛

North Sea

DENMARK
Copenhagen

NETHERLANDS
⊛ Amsterdam

• Hamburg

Berlin ⊛

Brussels

BELGIUM

Rhine River

GERMANY

LUXEMBOURG

Prague ⊛

CZECH REPUBLIC

Danube River

Bern ⊛

SWITZERLAND

LIECHTENSTEIN

Vienna ⊛

AUSTRIA

SLOVENIA

Ljubljana ⊛

SAN MARINO

MONACO

Corsica (France)

ITALY

VATICAN CITY

⊛ Rome

• Naples

Sardinia (Italy)

Sicily

⊛ Valletta

MALTA

Mediterranean Sea

NORWAY

SWEDEN

FINLAND

Helsinki ⊛

• St. Petersburg

⊛ Tallinn
ESTONIA

Baltic Sea

LATVIA
Riga ⊛

LITHUANIA

KALININGRAD (Russia)

⊛ Vilnius

⊛ Minsk

BELARUS

Warsaw ⊛

POLAND

• Kraków

SLOVAKIA
⊛ Bratislava

⊛ Budapest

HUNGARY

⊛ Zagreb

CROATIA

BOSNIA AND HERZEGOVINA

Sarajevo ⊛

SERBIA AND MONTENEGRO

⊛ Belgrade

Danube River

Podgorica ⊛

⊛ Skopje
MACEDONIA

Tirana ⊛

ALBANIA

GREECE

⊛ Athens

Crete

RUSSIA

⊛ Moscow

Volga River

Volgograd •

UKRAINE

⊛ Kiev

MOLDOVA

Chişinău ⊛

ROMANIA

⊛ Bucharest

BULGARIA
⊛ Sofia

Black Sea

Istanbul •

⊛ Ankara

TURKEY

⊛ Nicosia

CYPRUS

KAZAKHSTAN

Caspian Sea

GEORGIA
T'bilisi ⊛

Baku ⊛

AZERBAIJAN

ASIA

◀ Inspectors examine cheese at a market in the **Netherlands**. Europe is famous for its cheeses.

▲ These girls are dressed for a festival in **Spain**. Such celebrations keep folk traditions alive.

A

Africa

Elephants lumber across the grasslands. Gorillas groom each other in a mountain forest. Hippopotamuses swim in a river. Amazing animals are just part of what Africa has to offer. You can also visit a busy, modern city such as Nairobi, in Kenya; see how diamonds are mined in South Africa; shop in colorful, outdoor markets; take a sailboat ride past temples on the Nile; and climb some of the world's highest sand dunes in Earth's biggest hot desert. It's called the Sahara.

Jambo! Beautiful beadwork is part of a Masai girl's traditional dress. I live in Kenya where elephants like these roam free. In the distance stands Kilimanjaro, the highest peak in Africa. You can find it on the map on the next page.

Africa

The Land

 Land regions Most of Africa is a high, flat plateau. There are few mountains. The Sahara and the Kalahari are among its largest deserts. Rain forests grow along the Equator. Grasslands cover most of the rest of the continent.

▲ **Victoria Falls,** on the Zambezi River, is one of Africa's wonders. Its African name means "smoke that thunders."

Water The Nile and the Congo are Africa's longest rivers. Most of Africa's largest lakes are in the Great Rift Valley.

◄ Zebras live on grasslands called savannas near the **Equator**. No two zebras have exactly the same pattern of stripes.

Climate The Equator crosses Africa's middle, so many places on the continent are hot. It is always wet in the rain forest. Much of the rest of Africa has wet and dry seasons.

Plants Thorny trees called acacias provide food and shade for grassland animals. Date palms grow around desert water holes. Mahogany is one of many kinds of rain forest trees.

▲ Giant sand dunes in the **Sahara** tower high above this jeep. This huge desert covers most of northern Africa.

Animals Some of Africa's most familiar animals are shown here. There are also lions and many kinds of antelopes. Lemurs live on Madagascar, Africa's largest island.

◄ Hot springs boil on the shores of a lake in the **Great Rift Valley**. This is actually a series of valleys that run through the eastern part of the continent.

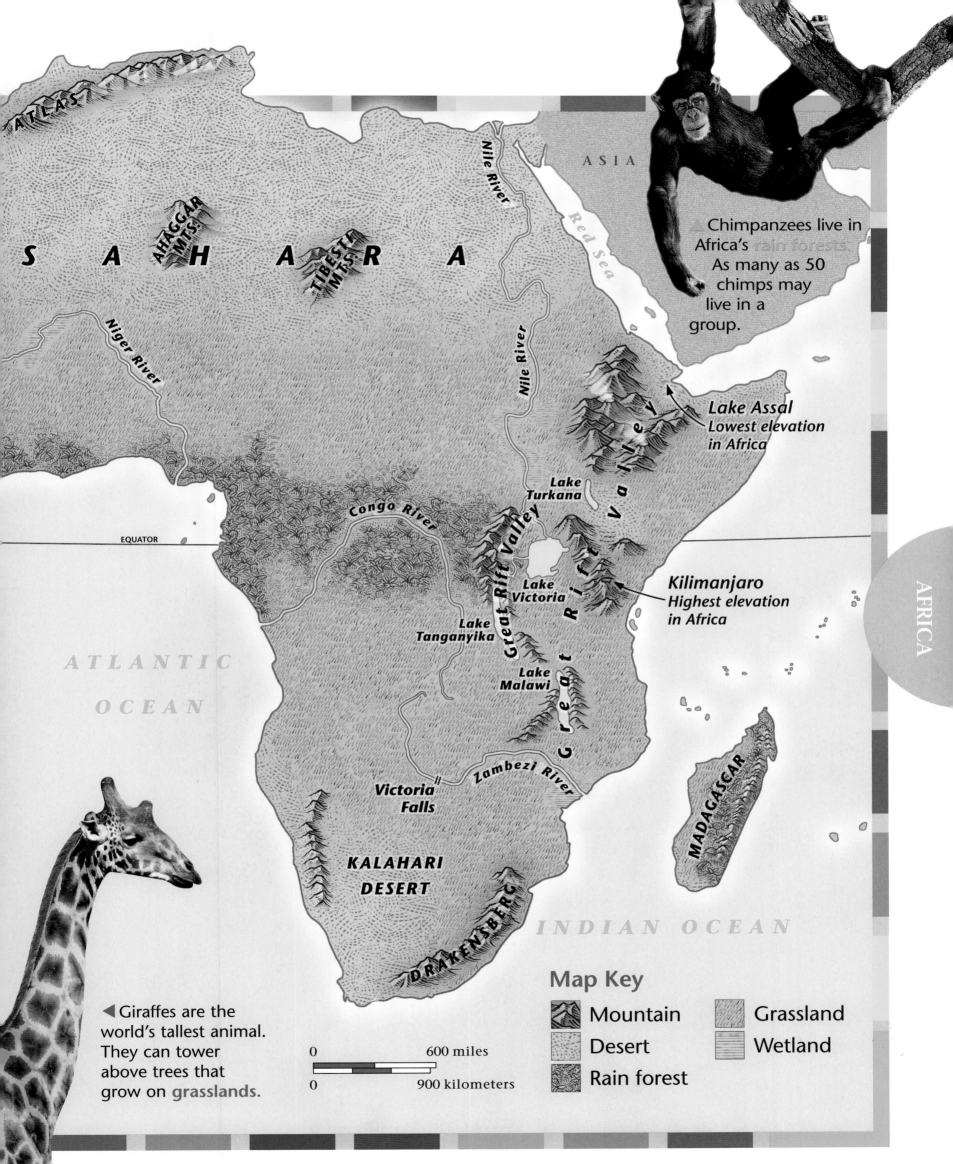

ATLAS

S A H A R A

AHAGGAR MTS.

TIBESTI MTS.

Niger River

Nile River

Nile River

ASIA

Red Sea

Chimpanzees live in Africa's rain forests. As many as 50 chimps may live in a group.

Lake Assal
Lowest elevation in Africa

EQUATOR

Congo River

Great Rift Valley

Great Rift Valley

Lake Turkana

Lake Victoria

Lake Tanganyika

Kilimanjaro
Highest elevation in Africa

Lake Malawi

ATLANTIC

OCEAN

MADAGASCAR

Zambezi River

Victoria Falls

KALAHARI DESERT

DRAKENSBERG

INDIAN OCEAN

◄ Giraffes are the world's tallest animal. They can tower above trees that grow on grasslands.

0   600 miles

0   900 kilometers

Map Key

Mountain

Desert

Rain forest

Grassland

Wetland

Africa

◀ These boys are picking dates. **Algeria** is a leading producer of this fruit.

 Countries Most of Africa's 53 countries were ruled by European countries from the late 1800s to the 1960s. Sudan has the most land. Nigeria has the most people.

Cities Cairo and Kinshasa are Africa's biggest cities. Both are on large rivers near the coast. More people live in villages and on farms than in cities.

▲ **Harare** is Zimbabwe's capital. It is one of the many modern cities in Africa.

People People in northern Africa's largest countries are mostly Arabs. Most black Africans live south of the Sahara in hundreds of different ethnic groups. Most Europeans live in South Africa.

Languages Arabic is spoken in the north. Native languages are spoken south of the Sahara. English, French, and Portuguese are the main European languages.

▲ Small sailboats called feluccas carry goods to trade along the Nile. This river is the longest in Africa.

Products Africa is a leading producer of cocoa beans, gold, diamonds, and petroleum.

▶ The Sphinx and the pyramid behind it were built by people who lived in **Egypt** thousands of years ago.

Canary Islands (Spain)

WESTERN SAHARA (Morocco)

MAURITANI

Nouakchott ⊛
CAPE VERDE
Praia ⊛   Dakar ⊛   SENEGAL
Banjul ⊛
GAMBIA   Bamako
Bissau ⊛
GUINEA-BISSAU   GUINEA
Conakry ⊛
Freetown ⊛
SIERRA LEONE   LIBERIA
Monrovia ⊛

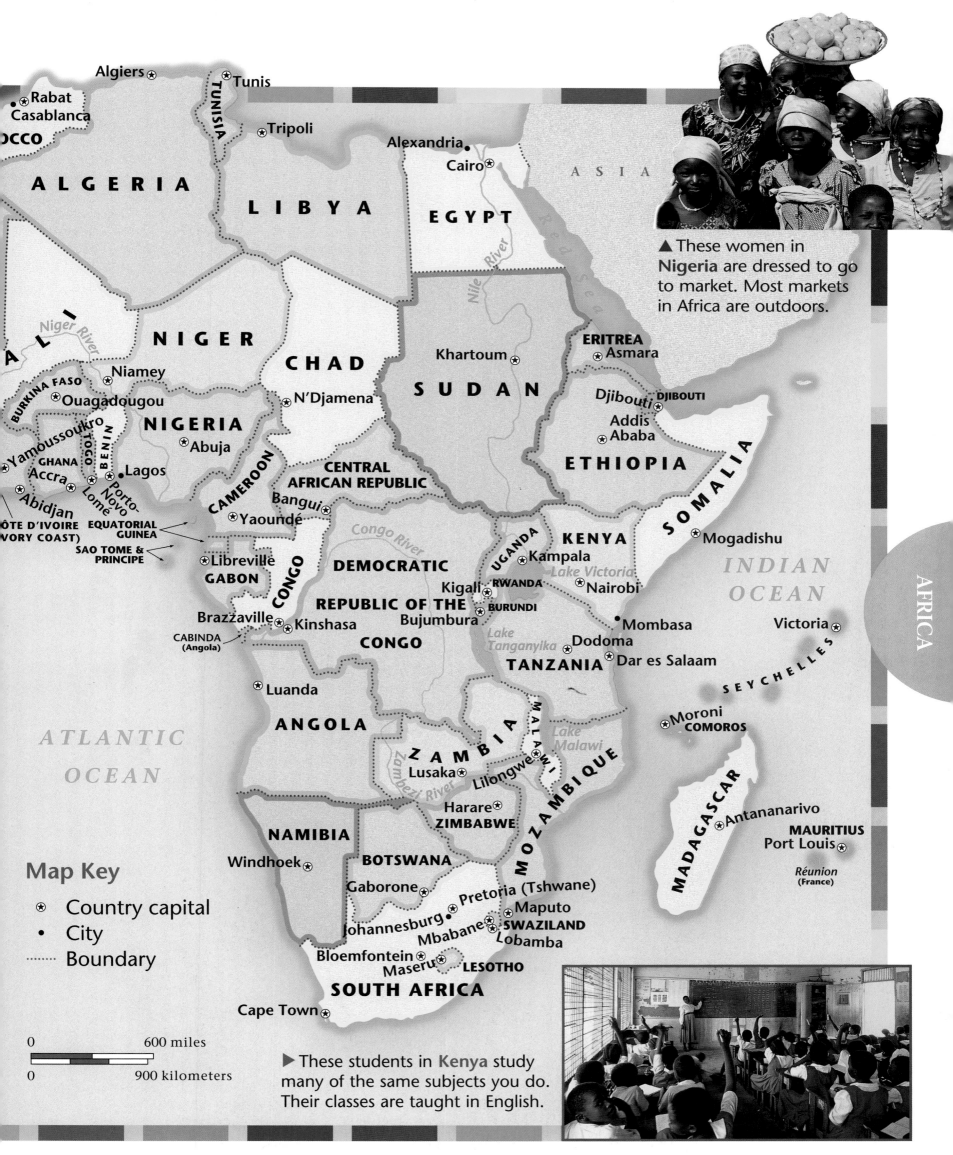

Algiers ⊛

Rabat ⊛
Casablanca •
OCCO

•Tunis

TUNISIA

•Tripoli

ALGERIA

LIBYA

Alexandria•
Cairo ⊛

EGYPT

ASIA

Red Sea

Nile River

▲ These women in **Nigeria** are dressed to go to market. Most markets in Africa are outdoors.

MALI

Niger River

NIGER

Niamey •

BURKINA FASO
Ouagadougou •
Yamoussoukro •
GHANA   BENIN   TOGO
Accra •   Lomé   Porto-
CÔTE D'IVOIRE   Novo
(IVORY COAST)
EQUATORIAL
GUINEA
SAO TOME &
PRINCIPE

Abidjan •

Lagos •

NIGERIA
⊛ Abuja

CHAD

N'Djamena •

Khartoum ⊛

SUDAN

ERITREA
Asmara ⊛

Djibouti • DJIBOUTI
Addis
Ababa •

ETHIOPIA

CENTRAL
AFRICAN REPUBLIC

Bangui •
⊛ Yaoundé

CAMEROON

Congo River

SOMALIA

Mogadishu •

Libreville ⊛

GABON

CONGO

DEMOCRATIC

REPUBLIC OF THE

Brazzaville ⊛ • Kinshasa

CONGO

CABINDA
(Angola)

UGANDA
Kampala ⊛

Kigali ⊛
RWANDA
BURUNDI
Bujumbura •

KENYA

Lake Victoria
Nairobi •

Lake
Tanganyika
Dodoma ⊛

Mombasa •

INDIAN
OCEAN

Victoria ⊛

AFRICA

TANZANIA
• Dar es Salaam

SEYCHELLES

Luanda ⊛

ANGOLA

ATLANTIC
OCEAN

Zambezi River

ZAMBIA

Lusaka ⊛

MALAWI

Lake
Malawi

Lilongwe ⊛

MOZAMBIQUE

Moroni ⊛
COMOROS

Harare ⊛
ZIMBABWE

MADAGASCAR

Antananarivo •

MAURITIUS
Port Louis ⊛

NAMIBIA

Windhoek ⊛

BOTSWANA

Gaborone ⊛

Pretoria (Tshwane) ⊛

Maputo ⊛

Réunion
(France)

Map Key

⊛   Country capital

•   City

......   Boundary

Johannesburg •

Mbabane ⊛ SWAZILAND
Lobamba

Bloemfontein ⊛

Maseru ⊛ LESOTHO

SOUTH AFRICA

Cape Town • ⊛

0   600 miles

0   900 kilometers

▶ These students in **Kenya** study many of the same subjects you do. Their classes are taught in English.

Asia

Asia is Earth's largest continent. Mount Everest, the world's highest mountain, is here. Asia also has some of the world's longest rivers, biggest deserts, and thickest forests. The Dead Sea is the lowest place on the continent. It is called "dead" because its water is too salty for fish and other animals to live in. More people live in Asia than anywhere else. The world's very first cities were built along river valleys in Asia long, long ago.

Namasté! I'm from Nepal. In mountainous countries like mine, farmers cut wide steps called terraces into hillsides to make flat land to grow crops on. Rice grows on these terraces in Indonesia.

Asia

The Land

Land regions Much of Asia is a rolling plain covered by grasslands, forests, and tundra. The Himalaya and other high mountains stretch across the south. Deserts cover much of southwestern and central Asia.

Water Asia has huge rivers and lakes. The Yangtze is the longest river. The Caspian Sea (partly in Europe) is the world's largest saltwater lake. Lake Baikal is the world's deepest lake.

Climate Northern Asia has long, icy winters and short cool summers. Most of southern Asia is warm year-round with heavy summer rains.

Plants Areas of coniferous forest called taiga stretch across the north. The central grasslands are known as the Steppes. Rain forests grow in the southeast.

Animals Tigers, giant pandas, and cobras live in the wild only in Asia.

◀ A climber stands at the top of a peak in the **Himalaya.** Mount Everest rises in front of him.

▲ The Three Gorges Dam helps control flooding along the Yangtze River, in China.

▼ Children ride camels along a road in Rajasthan, a **desert** region in India east of the Indus River.

Mediterranean Sea

Black Sea

CAUCASUS MTS.

Caspian Sea

Dead Sea
Lowest elevation
in Asia

Persian Gulf

ARABIAN PENINSULA

Arabian Sea

AFRICA

0	600 miles
0	900 kilometers

ARCTIC OCEAN

Bering Sea

EUROPE

EUROPE-ASIA BOUNDARY

URAL MOUNTAINS

THE STEPPES

Aral Sea

Ob River

Irtysh River

Yenisey River

Lena River

Amur River

Lake Baikal

TIAN SHAN

GOBI

Yellow River

HIMALAYA

Indus River

Brahmaputra

Ganges River

Mt. Everest
Highest elevation in Asia

Yangtze River

Mekong River

Bay of Bengal

PACIFIC OCEAN

South China Sea

EQUATOR

New Guinea

Sumatra

Borneo

INDIAN OCEAN

AUSTRALIA

▲ Boys play in a **rain forest** in Indonesia. These forests grow throughout Southeast Asia, where winds called monsoons

Map Key

- Mountain
- Desert
- Coniferous forest
- Deciduous forest
- Rain forest
- Grassland
- Wetland
- Tundra

▼ A herder leads his reindeer past taiga, a kind of **coniferous forest.** Forests like this are found throughout northern Asia.

▶ Giant pandas live only in leafy bamboo forests that grow on **mountains** in southwestern China.

ASIA

Asia

The People

Countries Asia has 46 countries. China is the largest country with boundaries entirely in Asia. Russia takes up the most area, but it is counted as part of Europe (*see pages 36–37*). Indonesia is Asia's largest island country.

Cities Much of Asia is too high, too dry, or too cold for people to live in. Most cities are near the coast or along busy rivers. Tokyo, in Japan, is the largest city.

People Asia has more people than any other continent. Each ethnic group has its own language, customs, and appearance. Most people work as farmers or fishermen.

Languages So many languages are spoken in Asia that even neighbors can have trouble understanding each other. India, for example, has 16 official languages!

Products Asia's chief products include rice, wheat, petroleum, cotton, rubber, tea, motor vehicles, and computers.

▲ **Hong Kong** is one of Asia's busiest trading centers. It is a special province of China.

◄ This boy in **Shanghai** draws symbols used in writing the Chinese language. Each symbol stands for a word or an idea.

EUROPE

Istanbul
Ankara
T'bilisi
GEORGIA
ARMENIA
Yerevan
TURKEY
LEBANON
Beirut
SYRIA
Damascus
AZERBAIJAN
Jerusalem
ISRAEL
Amman
JORDAN
Baghdad
Tehran
IRAQ
I R
KUWAIT
Kuwait
SAUDI
BAHRAIN
Riyadh
QATAR
Doha
Abu
Dh
A R A B I A
UNITED ARAB
EMIRATES
Musca
Sanaa
Y E M E N
OMAN
RUSSIA
Mediterranean Sea
Black Sea
Red Sea
AFRICA

▼ This young boy works in a spice market. In **India** people mix lots of spices together to make a strong flavor called curry.

0   600 miles
0   900 kilometers

► This masked dancer is from Bali. Bali is one of more than 3,000 islands that make up the country of **Indonesia**.

ARCTIC OCEAN

New Siberian Islands

North Land

Novaya Zemlya

Bering *Sea*

▶ Water buffaloes, like this one in Vietnam, are used for pulling plows in rice fields. Rice is Asia's most important food crop.

EUROPE-ASIA BOUNDARY

Moscow

R U S S I A

Ob' River

Irtysh River

Yenisey River

Lena River

Amur River

Lake Baikal

Sakhalin

PACIFIC OCEAN

Astana ⊛

K A Z A K H S T A N

Aral Sea

Ulaanbaatar ⊛

Harbin •

JAPAN

⊛ Tokyo
• Yokohama

UZBEKISTAN

M O N G O L I A

Shenyang •

NORTH KOREA

URKMENISTAN Bishkek
Tashkent ⊛ KYRGYZSTAN

Beijing ⊛

Pyongyang ⊛
⊛ Seoul

ngabat

⊛ Dushanbe
TAJIKISTAN

SOUTH KOREA

AFGHANISTAN

Yellow River

Xi'an •

Shanghai •

Map Key

Kabul ⊛

C H I N A

⊛ Country capital

⊛ Islamabad

Indus River

Chengdu •

Yangtze River

• Wuhan

• City

PAKISTAN Delhi •

Brahmaputra River

Chongqing •

⊛ Taipei

········· Boundary

New Delhi ⊛

N E P A L

Thimphu ⊛
BHUTAN

TAIWAN
The People's Republic of China
claims Taiwan as its 23rd province.

Karachi •

Kathmandu ⊛

Ganges River

BANGLADESH
⊛ Dhaka

• Hong Kong

n

Kolkata
(Calcutta) •

• Hanoi

Mumbai •
(Bombay)

I N D I A

MYANMAR
(BURMA)

LAOS

Hainan

⊛ Manila

Bay of Bengal

⊛ Vientiane

South China Sea

PHILIPPINES

Philippine Sea

Yangon ⊛
(Rangoon)

THAILAND

VIETNAM

• Chennai
(Madras)

Bangkok ⊛

CAMBODIA

Phnom
Penh ⊛ • Ho Chi
Minh City

SRI LANKA

Bandar Seri Begawan

New Guinea

MALDIVES
Male ⊛

• Colombo

BRUNEI ⊛

MALAYSIA

M A L A Y S

Kuala Lumpur ⊛

Borneo

*Sulawesi
(Celebes)*

SINGAPORE

Sumatra

I N D O N E S I A

INDIAN
OCEAN

Jakarta ⊛
Java

Bali

Dili •
TIMOR-LESTE
(EAST TIMOR)

AUSTRALIA

▶ This pipeline carries oil from Saudi Arabia to tanker ships in the Persian Gulf.

ASIA

ASIA **49**

Australia

Australia is a most unusual place. It is Earth's smallest and flattest continent and one of the driest, too. It has many large deserts. "Aussies," as Australians like to call themselves, nicknamed their continent "the land down under." That's because the entire continent lies south of, or "under," the Equator. Most Australians live in cities along the coast. But Australia also has huge cattle and sheep ranches. Many ranch children live far from school. They get their lessons by mail or from the Internet or the radio. Their doctors even visit by airplane!

Awa! I'm an Aborigine, one of Australia's native people. My face is painted for a special ceremony. The giant rock behind me is sacred to my people. We call it Uluru. You might know it as Ayers Rock.

AUSTRALIA

Australia

The Land

▲ Limestone towers rise above a **desert** in Western Australia. Desert covers much of the continent.

![mountain icon] **Land regions** The Great Dividing Range stretches along the east coast and into Tasmania. Most of the rest of Australia is a plateau covered by grasslands and deserts.

![water icon] **Water** The Darling, Australia's longest river, is dry during part of the year. So is Lake Eyre, the continent's largest lake. Water lies underground in the Great Artesian Basin.

![sun icon] **Climate** Most of the continent is very dry. Winds called monsoons bring heavy seasonal rains to the northern coast. Southern Australia can be cold in winter, but much of the continent is warm year-round.

▲ A school of fish swims past the **Great Barrier Reef.** It is the world's largest coral reef.

![leaf icon] **Plants** Eucalyptuses, or gum trees, and acacias are the most common kinds of plants. They grow throughout Australia.

![turtle icon] **Animals** Australia has many unusual mammals. Koalas and kangaroos raise their young in pouches on their bellies. The platypus is a mammal that has a bill like a duck's. Its babies hatch from eggs.

▲ Moss covers trees and logs in a forest in Tasmania. This island has a much wetter climate than most of mainland Australia.

▶ Koalas live only in **eucalyptus forests.** At one time koalas almost became extinct. Now they are protected by strict laws.

Hamersley Range

Darling Range

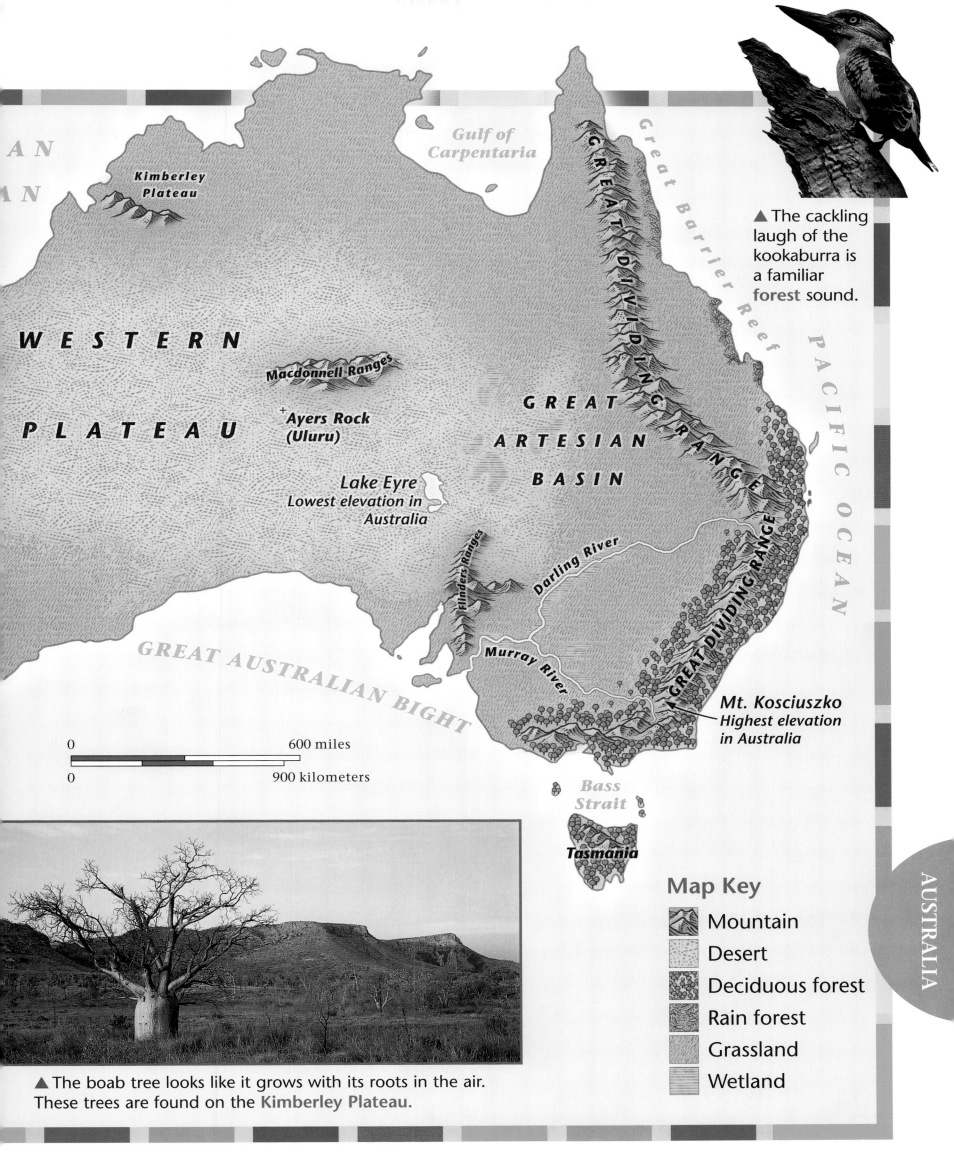

Gulf of Carpentaria

Kimberley Plateau

WESTERN PLATEAU

Macdonnell Ranges

⁺Ayers Rock (Uluru)

Lake Eyre
Lowest elevation in Australia

GREAT ARTESIAN BASIN

GREAT DIVIDING RANGE

Great Barrier Reef

PACIFIC OCEAN

▲ The cackling laugh of the kookaburra is a familiar **forest** sound.

Flinders Ranges

Darling River

Murray River

▲ GREAT DIVIDING RANGE

Mt. Kosciuszko
Highest elevation in Australia

GREAT AUSTRALIAN BIGHT

0		600 miles
0		900 kilometers

Bass Strait

Tasmania

Map Key

⬛ Mountain
⬛ Desert
⬛ Deciduous forest
⬛ Rain forest
⬛ Grassland
⬛ Wetland

▲ The boab tree looks like it grows with its roots in the air. These trees are found on the **Kimberley Plateau**.

Australia

The People

Countries Australia is the only continent that is also a country. It is divided into six states—including Tasmania—and two territories.

▲ Surfing is a popular sport in Australia. There is a city near **Brisbane** named Surfers Paradise.

Cities All the chief cities are near the coast— even the capital, Canberra. Sydney has the most people, followed by Melbourne, Brisbane, and Perth.

◄A monorail zips people around **Sydney.** The city is a busy port and the capital of the state of New South Wales.

People Most Australians are descendants of settlers from the United Kingdom and Ireland. Aborigines came to Australia from Asia some 40,000 years ago.

▼ Cafés, like this one, can be hundreds of miles apart in the **outback.** Few people live in this dry, central region.

Languages English is the main language of Australia. Aborigines speak some 250 different languages.

Products Australia's chief products include wool, beef, wheat, fruits, bauxite, coal, uranium, and diamonds. Most manufactured goods are imported.

◄The world's largest cultured pearls are grown in oyster beds along Australia's **northern coast.**

IND
OCE

Port Hedland

Perth⊙

Darwin

Gulf of
Carpentaria

NORTHERN
TERRITORY

Cairns

Townsville

Mount Isa

Alice
Springs

QUEENSLAND

A U S T R A L I A

WESTERN

AUSTRALIA

Mackay

PACIFIC
OCEAN

Rockhampton

SOUTH

AUSTRALIA

Lake
Eyre

Brisbane

Gold
Coast

Darling River

NEW SOUTH

WALES

GREAT AUSTRALIAN BIGHT

Adelaide

KANGAROO I.

Murray River

Sydney

Canberra

AUSTRALIAN
CAPITAL
TERRITORY

VICTORIA

Melbourne

PACIFIC
OCEAN

Map Key

⊛ Country capital

⊙ State or territory capital

• City

······ State boundary

0   600 miles
0   900 kilometers

TASMANIA

Hobart

▲ This family lives on
a farm in **Queensland**,
where wheat is an
important product.

◀ This Aborigine is playing a wooden
pipe called a didgeridoo. Many of
Australia's native people live in
the **Northern Territory**.

▼ Australia has huge
cattle farms called
stations. Some of
the largest are in
Western Australia.

Antarctica

Brrrr! Antarctica takes first place as the coldest continent. It is the land around the South Pole. An ice cap two miles thick in places covers most of the land. Temperatures rarely get above freezing. It is also the only continent that has no countries. It has research stations but no cities. The only people are scientists, explorers, and tourists. Everyone stays for awhile, then goes home. The largest land animals that live here year-round are a few kinds of insects!

Chances are you'll see more penguins than people if you visit Antarctica. Like the whale behind them, Penguins depend on the ocean for food. They come ashore to have their babies.

Antarctica

The Land

▲ This strong-sided ship is an icebreaker. It cuts a path through ice in the **Ross Sea**.

 Land regions The Transantarctic Mountains divide the continent into two parts. East Antarctica, where the South Pole is located, is mostly a high, flat, icy area. West Antarctica is mountainous. Vinson Massif is the highest peak.

Water Most of Earth's fresh water is frozen in Antarctica's ice cap. The ice breaks off when it meets the sea. These huge floating chunks of ice in the ocean are called icebergs.

Climate Antarctica is windy and dry. It gets very little snow. Most of the snow that falls turns to ice. The thick ice cap has built up over millions of years.

▲ Few people have ever climbed Antarctica's mountains. This one is called "the Razor." It is near the coast in **Queen Maud Land**.

Plants Billions of tiny plants live in the surrounding oceans. Mosses and lichens grow on the land.

Animals Penguins and other seabirds nest on the coast. Whales, seals, and tiny shrimplike animals called krill live in the oceans.

▼ Elephant seals come ashore along the rocky **Antarctic Peninsula** during the summer.

◄ Jellyfish grow very large under the **sea ice** around the continent. Here they have few enemies so they live a long time.

ATLANTIC OCEAN

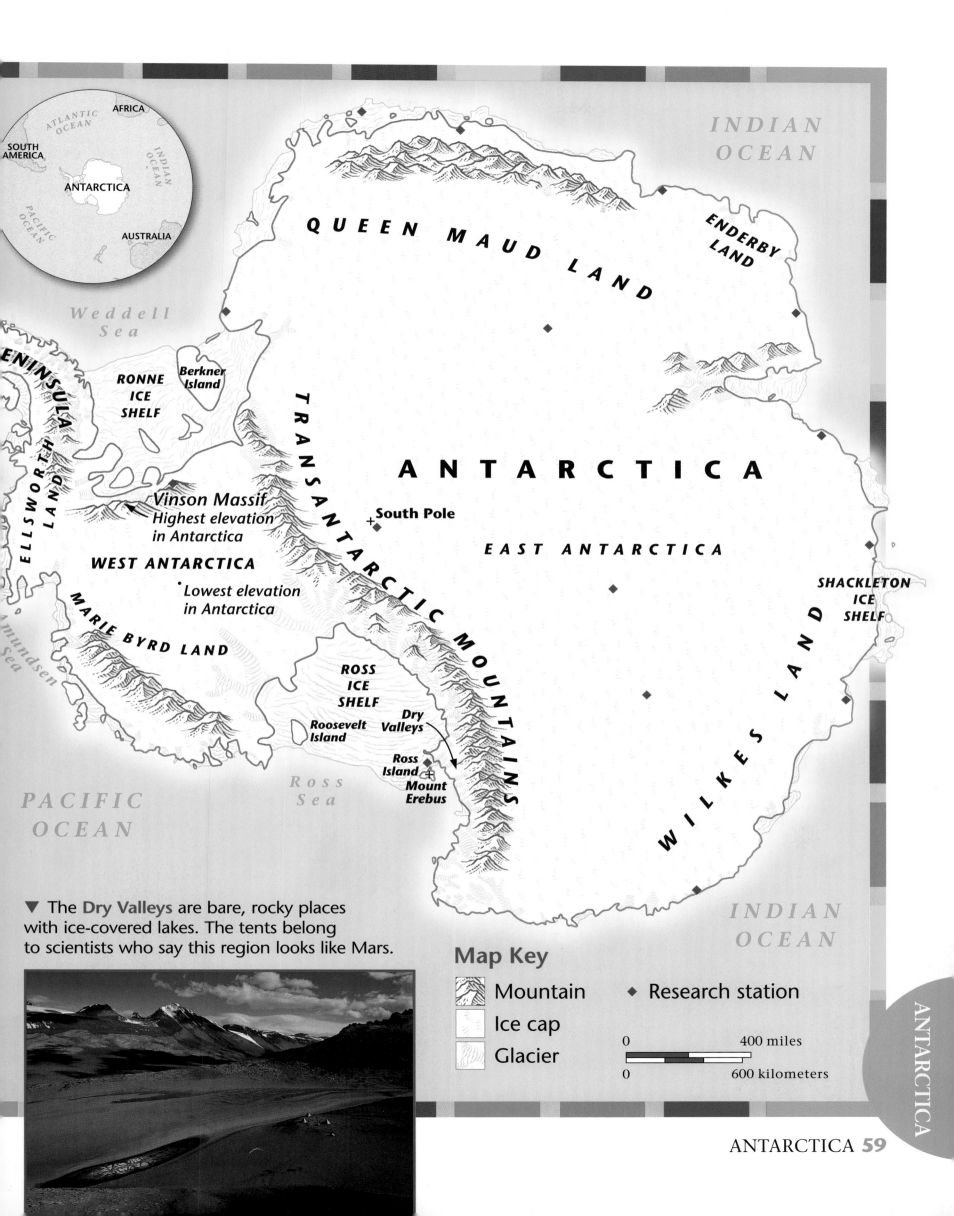

INDIAN OCEAN

AFRICA

ATLANTIC OCEAN

SOUTH AMERICA

INDIAN OCEAN

ANTARCTICA

PACIFIC OCEAN

AUSTRALIA

QUEEN MAUD LAND

ENDERBY LAND

Weddell Sea

RONNE ICE SHELF

Berkner Island

ANTARCTICA

Vinson Massif
Highest elevation in Antarctica

+ South Pole

EAST ANTARCTICA

PENINSULA

ELLSWORTH LAND

WEST ANTARCTICA

· *Lowest elevation in Antarctica*

SHACKLETON ICE SHELF

MARIE BYRD LAND

Amundsen Sea

TRANSANTARCTIC MOUNTAINS

ROSS ICE SHELF

Roosevelt Island

Dry Valleys

Ross Island

Mount Erebus

Ross Sea

WILKES LAND

PACIFIC OCEAN

INDIAN OCEAN

▼ The **Dry Valleys** are bare, rocky places with ice-covered lakes. The tents belong to scientists who say this region looks like Mars.

Map Key

⛰ Mountain   ◆ Research station

Ice cap

Glacier

0   400 miles

0   600 kilometers

World at a Glance

Land

The Continents, Largest to Smallest

1. **Asia:** 17,213,300 sq mi *(44,579,000 sq km)*
2. **Africa:** 11,609,000 sq mi *(30,065,000 sq km)*
3. **North America:** 9,449,500 sq mi *(24,474,000 sq km)*
4. **South America:** 6,880,500 sq mi *(17,819,000 sq km)*
5. **Antarctica:** 5,100,400 sq mi *(13,209,000 sq km)*
6. **Europe:** 3,837,400 sq mi *(9,938,000 sq km)*
7. **Australia:** 2,969,906 sq mi *(7,692,024 sq km)*

Water

The Oceans, Largest to Smallest

1. **Pacific Ocean:** 65,436,246 sq mi *(169,479,100 sq km)*
2. **Atlantic Ocean:** 35,338,040 sq mi *(91,526,400 sq km)*
3. **Indian Ocean:** 29,829,823 sq mi *(74,694,800 sq km)*
4. **Arctic Ocean:** 5,390,024 sq mi *(13,960,100 sq km)*

Highest, Longest, Largest

The numbers below show locations on the map.

❶ **Highest Mountain on a Continent**
Mt. Everest, in Asia: 29,035 ft *(8,850 m)*

❷ **Largest Island**
Greenland, in the Atlantic Ocean: 840,065 sq mi *(2,175,600 sq km)*

❸ **Largest Ocean**
Pacific Ocean: 65,436,246 sq mi *(169,479,100 sq km)*

❹ **Longest River**
Nile River, in Africa: 4,241 mi *(6,825 km)*

❺ **Largest Freshwater Lake**
Lake Superior, in North America: 31,701 sq mi *(82,100 sq km)*

❻ **Largest Saltwater Lake**
Caspian Sea, in Europe-Asia: 143,254 sq mi *(371,000 sq km)*

❼ **Largest Hot Desert**
Sahara, in Africa: 3,475,000 sq mi *(9,000,000 sq km)*

❽ **Largest Cold Desert**
Antarctica: 5,100,400 sq mi *(13,209,000 sq km)*

People

More than 6 billion people live on the Earth—enough to fill a string of school buses that would circle the Equator almost 24 times! More than half the world's people live in Asia.

Five Largest Countries by Number of People

1. **China, Asia:** 1,300,060,000 people
2. **India, Asia:** 1,086,640,000 people
3. **United States, North America:** 293,633,000 people
4. **Indonesia, Asia:** 218,746,000 people
5. **Brazil, South America:** 179,091,000 people

Five Largest Cities* by Number of People

1. **Tokyo, Japan (Asia):** 12,360,000 people
2. **Mumbai, India (Asia):** 11,914,400 people
3. **São Paulo, Brazil (South America):** 10,434,300 people
4. **Moscow, Russia (Europe):** 10,101,500 people
5. **Delhi, India (Asia):** 9,817,400 people

*Figures are for city proper, not metropolitan area

Glossary

bauxite a substance mined from the Earth that is the chief source of aluminum

capital city a place where a country's government is located

city a settled place where people work in jobs other than farming

coral reef a stony formation in warm, shallow ocean water that is made up of the skeletons of tiny sea animals called corals

country a place that has boundaries, a name, a flag, and a government that is the highest worldly authority over the land and the people who live there

environment the world around you, including people, cities, beliefs, plants and animals, air, water—everything

ethnic group people who share a common ancestry, language, beliefs, and traditions

European Union an organization of 25 European countries (Austria,* Belgium,* Cyprus, Czech Republic, Denmark, Estonia, Finland,* France,* Germany,* Greece,* Hungary, Ireland,* Italy,* Latvia, Lithuania, Luxembourg,* Malta, Netherlands,* Poland, Portugal,* Slovakia, Slovenia, Spain,* Sweden, and the United Kingdom)

glacier a large, slow-moving mass of ice; glaciers that cover huge areas are called ice caps

lemur an animal related to monkeys that is active at night and lives mostly in forests on Madagascar, in Africa

lichen a plantlike organism that is part alga and part fungus and that usually lives where few plants can survive

* The euro is the country's official currency.

mosses nonflowering, low-growing green plants that grow on rocks and trees throughout the world

outback the name Australians use for the dry interior region of their country where few people live

plains large areas of mainly flat land often covered with grasses

province a unit of government similar to a state

state a unit of government that takes up a specific area within a country, as in one of the 50 large political units in the United States

Steppes a Russian name for the grasslands that stretch from eastern Europe into Asia

taiga a Russian word for the scattered, coniferous forests that grow in cold, northern regions

Pronunciations

Note: Syllables printed in all capital letters should be accented.

Aborigine ah buh RIJ uh nee

Ayers ARZ

Baikal by KALL

bauxite BAWK site

boab BO ab

Buenos Aires bway nus AR eez

didgeridoo DIH juh ree doo

eucalyptus you kuh LIP tus

Eyre AR

felucca fuh LOO kuh

Harare hah RAH ray

Himalaya him AHL yah

Kalahari ka luh HAR ee

Kilimanjaro kih luh mun JAR o

Kinshasa kin SHAH suh

koala kuh WAH luh

Latvia LAT vee uh

lichen LIE kun

Liechtenstein LIKT un shtine

Maasai MAH sigh

Monaco MAH nuh ko

Nigeria nigh JIR ee uh

Quechua KEH chuh wuh

Rio de Janeiro REE oo dee zha NAY roo

San Marino san muh REE no

Sudan soo DAN

Sumatra suh MAH truh

taiga TIE guh

Tasmania taz MAY nee uh

Uluru oo LOO roo

Yangtze yang SEE

Zambezi zam BEE zee

Zimbabwe zim BAH bway

Greetings in Native Languages

awa AH wuh
an Australian Aborigine word for a friendly "hello"

imaynalla ee my NAH yuh
"greetings" in Quechua, a Native American language of South America

kha hay kaw HAY
"greetings" in Crow, a Native American language of the United States

namasté no mo STAY
"I salute you" in Nepalese, the language of Nepal, in Asia

sveiks SVAYKS
"hello" in Latvian, the language of Latvia, a country in eastern Europe

jambo JAM bo
"hello" in Swahili, a language spoken throughout East Africa

Index

Pictures and the text that describes them have their page numbers printed in **bold** type.

National Geographic Society

John M. Fahey, Jr.
President and Chief Executive Officer

Gilbert M. Grosvenor
Chairman of the Board

Nina D. Hoffman
*Executive Vice President, President of Books and
Education Publishing Group*

Ericka Markman
*Senior Vice President, President of Children's Books
and Education Publishing Group*

Stephen Mico
*Senior Vice President and Publisher,
Children's Books and Education Publishing Group*

Staff for this book

Nancy Laties Feresten
*Vice President, Editor-in Chief
of Children's Books*

Suzanne Patrick Fonda
Project Editor

Marianne R. Koszorus
Bea Jackson
Art Directors

Carl Mehler
Director of Maps

Sharon Davis Thorpe
David M. Seager
Designers

Susan McGrath
Writer

Marilyn Mofford Gibbons
Margaret Sidlosky
Illustrations Editors

Jennifer Emmett
Associate Editor

Jo Tunstall
Priyanka Lamichhane
Editorial Assistants

Thomas L. Gray
Joseph F. Ochlak
Nicholas P. Rosenbach
Map Editors/Researchers

Stuart Armstrong
Tibor G. Tóth
Map Illustration

Michelle H. Picard
Map Production Manager

Stuart Armstrong
John S. Ballay
Tibor G. Tóth
Greg Ugiansky
Martin S. Walz
Map Production

Ann Ince-McKillop
Marcia Pires-Harwood
Text Research

Janet Dustin
Jean Cantu
Aaron Hubbard
Illustrations Assistants

Connie D. Binder
Indexer

Rebecca E. Hinds
Managing Editor

Jeff Reynolds
*Marketing Director
Children's Books*

Laurie J. Hembree
*Marketing Manager
Children's Books*

R. Gary Colbert
Production Director

Lewis R. Bassford
Production Manager

Vincent P. Ryan
Maryclare Tracy
Manufacturing Managers

Consultants

Osa Brand
*Educational Affairs Director
Association of American Geographers*

Peggy Steele Clay
*Teacher-in-Residence
National Geographic Society*

Jacki Vawter
*Specialist in Early
Childhood Education
Alexandria, Virginia*

Acknowledgements

We are grateful for the assistance
of John Agnone, Peggy Candore,
Alexander L. Cohn, Anne Marie
Houppert, Sandra Leonard, and
Lyle Rosbotham of the National
Geographic Book Division.

One of the world's
largest nonprofit
scientific and
educational
organizations, the
National Geographic Society was
founded in 1888 "for the increase
and diffusion of geographic
knowledge." Fulfilling this mission,
the Society educates and inspires
millions every day through its
magazine, books, television
programs, videos, maps and atlases,
research grants, the National
Geographic Bee, teacher
workshops, and innovative
classroom materials.

The Society is supported through
membership dues, charitable gifts,
and income from the sale of its
educational products. This support
is vital to National Geographic's
mission to increase global
understanding and promote
conservation through exploration,
research, and education.

For more information please call
1-800-NGS-LINE (647-5463) or
write to the following address:

NATIONAL GEOGRAPHIC SOCIETY
1145 17th Street N.W.
Washington, D.C. 20036-4688
U.S.A.

Visit the Society's Web site:
www.nationalgeographic.com

Illustrations Credits

Photographs are from Getty Images except where indicated by an asterisk (*)

All illustrated physical maps and accompanying icons by Stuart Armstrong

Cover globe and all locator globes digitally created by Tibor G. Tóth

Front Matter:
Ed Simpson 2 (top); Michael Scott 2 (bottom); Connie Coleman 3 (top left); Paul Chesley 3 (top right); James Martin 3 (center left); Art Wolfe 3 (center right); Nicholas DeVore III 3 (bottom)

Understanding Your World:
*Sally J. Bensusen/Visual Science Studio 4 (top art) and 5 (top left art); *Theophilus Britt Griswold 4–5 (bottom art) and 5 (top right art); *Hal Pierce: NASA Goddard Laboratory for Atmospheres, data from NOAA 6 (left); *Tibor G. Tóth 6–7 (art); John Warden 10 (left); Hugh Sitton 10 (center); Steven Weinberg 10 (left); Andrea Booher 11 (top); Greg Probst 11 (top center); *Stephen and Michele Vaughan Photography 11 (bottom center); Cosmo Condina 11 (bottom left); *Michael Nichols 11 (bottom center); Tom Bean 11 (bottom right); John Noble 14 (top left); A. Witte/C. Mahaney 14 (top right); Jack Dykinga 14 (center left); Bruno DeHogues 14 (center right); *Arvind Garg/Corbis 14 (bottom); Stuart McCall 15 (top left); Chad Ehlers 15 (top right); Martine Mouchy 15 (center); Mark Harris 15 (bottom)

North America:
Ed Simpson 16–17; Rosemary Calvert 16–17; Charles Krebs 18 (top); Stephen Krasemann 18 (top center); Mark Lewis 18 (bottom center); Bruce Wilson 18 (bottom left); James Randklev 18–19; Charles Krebs 19; Gary Brettnacher 20 (top); George Hunter 20 (top center); Mark Lewis 20 (bottom center); Cosmo Condina 20 (bottom center left); Nick Gunderson 20 (bottom left); *Alison Wright/Corbis 20 (bottom right); Will & Deni McIntyre 21; Billy Hustace 22 (top); Jake Rais 22 (center); * © David Young-Wolff/PhotoEdit 22 (bottom); Pete Seaward 23 (top); Philip H. Coblentz 23 (bottom left); Royalty-Free/Corbis 23 (bottom right); Tim Thompson 24 (top); Cosmo Condina 24 (center); *Mike Cassese/Reuters/Corbis 24 (bottom); Chris Thomaidis 25 (top); T. Davis/W. Bilenduke 25 (center); Wayne R. Bilenduke 25 (bottom)

South America:
Michael Scott 26; Tony Dawson 26–27; Nicholas DeVore III 28 (top); *James Holland 28 (top center); Bryan Parsley 28 (bottom center); Frans Lanting 28 (bottom); William J. Hebert 29; *Stuart Franklin 30 (top); Robert Frerck 30 (top center); *Heinz Kluetmeier/*SPORTS ILLUSTRATED 30 (bottom center); Robert Frerck 30 (bottom); *Don Kincaid 31 (top); Ary Diesendruck 31 (bottom)

Europe:
Connie Coleman 32; John Lawrence 32–33; James Balog 34 (top); Michael Busselle 34 (center); Art Wolfe 34 (bottom); Richard Passmore 34–5; *Bruce Coleman Ltd. 35; Jerry Alexander 36 (top); Yann Layma 36 (center); coins: *Fotosearch, paper money: *Medio IMages/Index Stock 36 (bottom left); Louis Grandadam 36 (bottom right); Maarten Udema 36–7; Anthony Cassidy 37

Africa:
James Martin 38; Renee Lynn 38–39; Chad Ehlers 40 (top); Kevin Schafer 40 (top center); Hugh Sitton 40 (bottom center); Michael Busselle 40 (bottom); Michael Busselle 40–41; Tim Davis 41; Will & Deni McIntyre 42 (top); Daniel May 42 (top center); Hugh Sitton 42 (bottom center); Sylvain Grandadam 42 (bottom); Sally Mayman 43 (top); Paul Kenward 43 (bottom)

Asia:
Nicholas DeVore III 44; *Gilbert M. Grosvenor/NGS Image Sales 44–45; Chris Noble 46 (top); *China Photos/Reuters/Corbis 46 (center); *Arvind Garg/Corbis 46 (bottom); James Nelson 47 (top); Paul Harris 47 (bottom left); Keren Su 47 (bottom right); *Walter Hodges/Corbis 48 (top); Michael Ventura 48 (center); Nicholas DeVore III 48 (bottom); *Kenneth Love 48–49; Keren Su 49 (top); Wayne Eastep 49 (bottom)

Australia:
Paul Chesley 50; Ed Collacott 50–51; Fred Bavendam 52 (top); Stuart Westmoreland 52 (top center); Grilly Bernard 52 (bottom center); Penny Tweedie 52 (bottom left); Sam Abell 53 (top); Oliver Strewe 53 (bottom); *Photo Index 54 (top); Matthew Lambert 54 (top center); Oliver Strewe 54 (bottom center); *David Doubilet 54 (bottom); David Austen 55 (top); Paul Souders 55 (bottom left); Robert Frerck 55 (bottom right)

Antarctica
Art Wolfe 56; Tim Davis 56–57; Kim Westerskov 58 (top); *Gordon Wiltsie 58 (center); *Norbert Wu 58 (bottom left); David Madison 58 (bottom right); *Maria Stenzel 59

Back cover:
Kevin Schafer (top left); Art Wolfe (top right); Masa Vemusi (bottom left); David Muench (bottom right)

The Library of Congress has cataloged the 1999 edition as follows:

National Geographic beginner's world atlas / photographs from Tony Stone Images
   p. cm.
   Includes index.
   Summary: Maps, photographs, illustrations, and text
present information about the continents of the world.

   1. Children's atlases. [1. Atlases. 2. Geography.] I. Title.
   II. Title: Beginner's world atlas
G1021 .N39 1999 <G&M>   CIP
912—dc21   MAPS

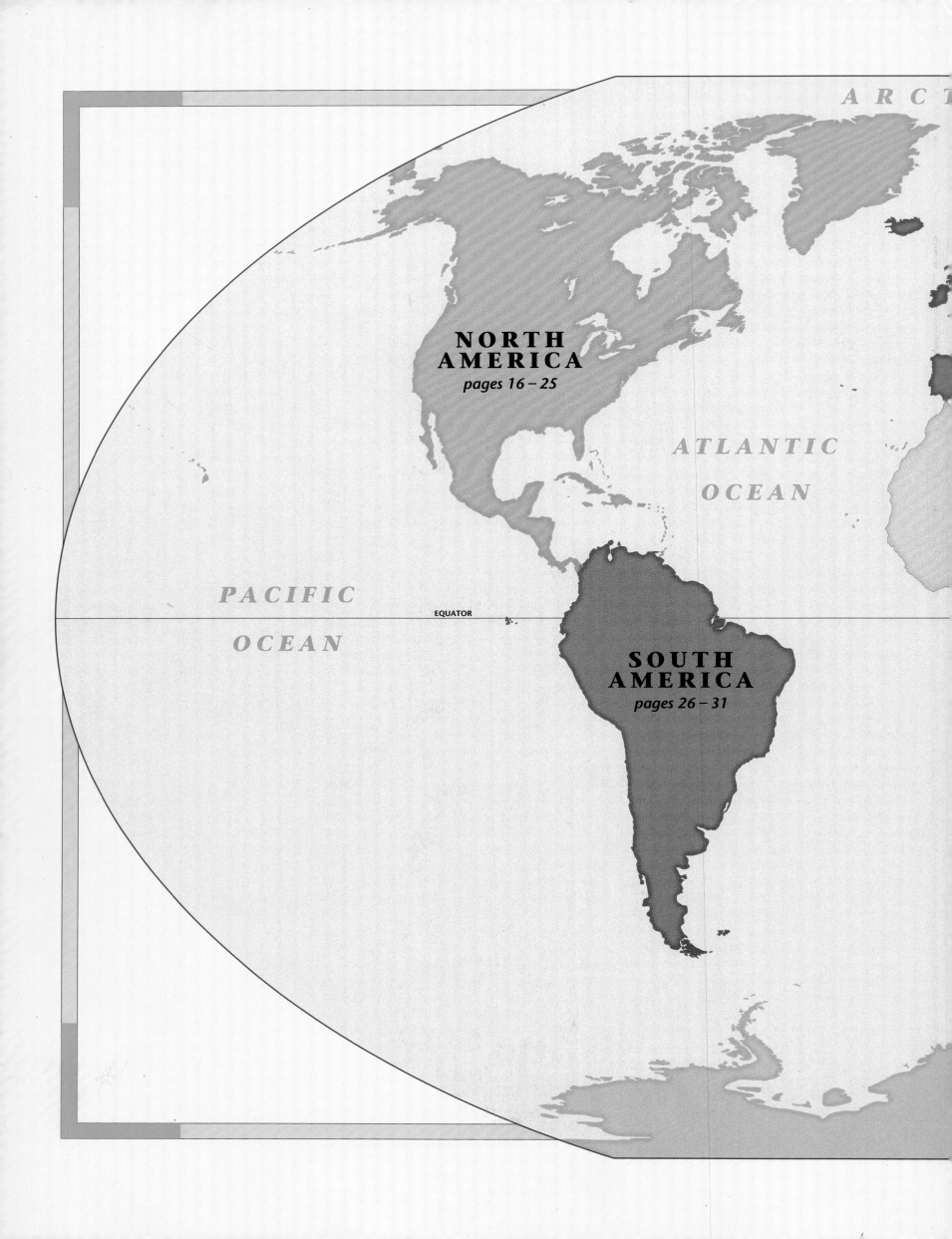

ARCT

NORTH
AMERICA
pages 16 – 25

ATLANTIC

OCEAN

PACIFIC

OCEAN

EQUATOR

SOUTH
AMERICA
pages 26 – 31